I.EE
5

D0177766

WATERFORD CITY AND
WITHDRAWN
LIBRARIES

A Child Called Freedom

ALSO BY CAROL LEE

To Die For
Crooked Angels
Good Grief
Talking Tough
The Blind Side of Eden
Friday's Child
The Ostrich Position

WATERFORD CITY AND COUNTY

WITHDRAWN

LIBRARY

A Child Called Freedom

Carol Lee

WATERFORD

No. 003833261

MUNICIPAL LIBRARY

C
CENTURY · LONDON

Published by Century in 2006

1 3 5 7 9 10 8 6 4 2

Copyright © Carol Lee 2006

Carol Lee has asserted her right under the Copyright, Designs and Patents Act,
1988 to be identified as the author of this work

This book is sold subject to the condition that it shall not, by way of trade or otherwise,
be lent, resold, hired out, or otherwise circulated without the publisher's prior consent in
any form of binding or cover other than that in which it is published and without a
similar condition including this condition being imposed on the subsequent purchaser

First published in the United Kingdom in 2006 by Century
The Random House Group Limited
20 Vauxhall Bridge Road, London SW1V 2SA

Random House Australia (Pty) Limited
20 Alfred Street, Milsons Point, Sydney,
New South Wales 2061, Australia

Random House New Zealand Limited
18 Poland Road, Glenfield
Auckland 10, New Zealand

Random House South Africa (Pty) Limited
Isle of Houghton, Corner of Boundary Road & Carse O'Gowrie,
Houghton 2198, South Africa

The Random House Group Limited Reg. No. 954009

www.randomhouse.co.uk

A CIP catalogue record for this book is available
from the British Library

Papers used by Random House are
natural, recyclable products made from wood grown in
sustainable forests. The manufacturing processes conform to
the environmental regulations of the country of origin

ISBN 1 8441 38747
ISBN-13 978 184413874 6

Typeset by Palimpsest Book Production Limited, Polmont, Stirlingshire
Printed and bound in Great Britain by Mackays of Chatham plc, Chatham, Kent

The author and publisher have made all reasonable efforts to contact copyright holders
for permission, and apologise for any omissions or errors in the form of credits given.
Corrections may be made to future printings.

To Freedom, Andile and the Class of '76

Contents

Contents

Photographs are by the author or from her family album, except the picture on page 110.

Preface
TWO ROADS

This is a book about connections, about a trail of chance events, encounters and journeys, the shape of which lies hidden for decades. Drawn together in the early years of this century, they nevertheless go back to one specific day thirty years ago – June 16th 1976.

On that day, a Wednesday at around 6 am, thousands of schoolchildren in an African township began to gather together for a large, orderly march.

They did not know at the time that their action would begin a long chain of violent events which would last for more than a decade. Neither did they know that within a few hours a number of them would be dead.

It was cold, mid-winter in South Africa, and some of the friends and classmates who gathered that morning had not had breakfast. They were game though, excited, ready to sing and dance on the March through Orlando West where a short statement of their grievances would be read out and delivered to the education offices.

The morning had begun much earlier for parents in Soweto

who rose soon after 4 am to prepare for a day's work in the factories, mines and suburban homes of the Big City, Johannesburg. They were servants in the main, although some had skilled and semi-skilled jobs in the manufacturing industry and in engineering in particular.

Most would set off for the 13-kilometre train journey with little to eat and would not have a meal until after their return home that evening, just ahead of nightfall. Unaware of what was planned that day, they went to work as usual.

This much of what history would name the Soweto Uprising, or the Soweto Children's Uprising, is known. After which the path, the story of this, one of the most significant events of the twentieth century, begins, imperceptibly at first, to diverge.

Small details to start with about whether people working in the city heard rumours and came home early. Then bigger divergences, not details this time, but crucial building blocks. Like who organised this event – and why. And what happened to them.

There are two stories, like two roads, when you try and approach Soweto – as if you are not meant to find your way. For the people in the townships in '76 lived in a peculiar and dangerous world where truth had been stood on its head. It had been upended for so long by this time, you wondered if it would ever stand up straight again.

In the courts of 'justice', people's skulls came into contact with police truncheons because 'your honour, he pushed his

head onto my baton'. The official language for pushing someone out of a top-floor window was 'he jumped, your worship'.

There was so much blood. And so many people fell from
the sky at nearby Johannesburg's notorious police headquarters, Blue Hotel, that truth lay curled up like a broken body
on the pavement.

It never went away though. Living deep, hidden, in certain
people, and recorded in words and photographs which
escaped the mad destroyers' attempts to torch the evidence,
burn the books, it lay wounded and waiting.

And while there is no one true story and no one set truth
about this or any other event, there is something vital about
uncurling the body of evidence from where it has lain broken
on the ground.

The narrative of why I, a relative stranger, should have
become involved in any of this unfolds in the following pages.
For this is a personal account and Soweto itself, a short while
back, is where we must begin.

Chapter One

BORDER CHILDREN

Carol and Sue in Africa

Soweto, September 2003

My journey into Soweto's story begins with words painted on stone, the sun of an African spring morning warming them and me. Beached in a small circle of gravel chips in the grounds of a museum, an above-head-high boulder has on its sides in white lettering the fact that this precinct commemorates the student uprising on June 16th 1976:

> On that day, in this vicinity, about 15,000 schoolchildren
> gathered . . . As the students marched peacefully . . .

armed police confronted them with gunfire.

In the wave of student resistance that followed throughout South Africa, at least 600 students died and thousands
were wounded. Thousands more were detained, tortured,
charged and imprisoned. Up to 12,000 fled the country.

The spirit and determination of the schoolchildren
resonated around the world, marking a turning point in the
struggle for freedom and democracy in South Africa.

At this site of national significance, the nation pays
homage to the students of 1976 who sacrificed their lives
so that the doors of learning and culture would be opened,
and South Africa could be free today.

This site unveiled on 16 June 2002.

Patterns, links can stay hidden for years and the woman
standing by my side in Soweto is my newly found cousin,
Sue. Her path and mine must have crisscrossed dozens of
times since we played as children some hundreds of miles
north of here. Yet we have met only once, briefly, since then.

What would we make of each other decades on, especially
in our family with its cupboards full of secrets, tragedies and
conflicting versions of events?

After years of hearing competing accounts from different
people at different times, I have come to believe them all.
Yes, the towering figure in our past, our English grandmother,
Nellie, was cruel-tongued, certainly to my mother and me.
And yes, she was a courageous, good woman too. But has

Sue been affected by the drama of our past, she on one side of a family divide, me on the other, Nellie inbetween?

Sue's mother, Joy, and my father, Vic, the oldest and youngest of Nellie's three children. Our grandmother, in feisty manner, took against the people all of her offspring married. But at least Sue's mother married an Englishman and it was my father's choice of a bride, my *Welsh* mother, Nellie disapproved of most. Not merely disapproval though, it was more like war, with the deep wounds of carefully depth-charged words not stopped till years after Nellie's death.

My father and Sue's mother seeing little of each other, the contradictory history has built up: Nellie as the good person in Sue's background and as the hurtful one in mine.

Different branches of the family, Sue and I look different, she with her father's Nordic looks, blonde and blue-eyed, me like my mother, Celtic and dark. Both tall, though, the same height. Family myths would have us opposite in temperament, Sue contained, me fiery, she responsible, me more wild. Yet we seem alike, just with different ways of expressing ourselves, Sue calm and measured, my heart worn more on my sleeve.

Both with passionate concerns about poverty and injustice, I learn of Sue's job as head of a charity working alongside Archbishop Tutu on the Truth and Reconciliation Commission (TRC), Sue and her colleagues taking care of witnesses travelling days to testify.

South Africa's unique way of dealing with its troubled past, the TRC's remit – to hear victims' evidence so their stories were on public record; to give limited amnesty to perpetrators who apologised for their deeds; to apportion financial reparation – the Commission meant many things to the thousands of people who appeared before it. Its basis, to encourage and allow truth-telling, to find where the bones were buried and lay them to rest, was an extraordinary venture and a long haul.

Having heard on the family grapevine of my early years in journalism, Sue hears first-hand about my own long haul – the books – the latest the story of my god-daughter Emma's battle with anorexia, her descent into illness and then, years later, asking me to write of her experience.

Meeting in a pub, Emma had 'adopted' me when she was not yet three years old, asking if I would read to her while her mother worked behind the bar.

'So, you see,' I say wryly, 'I'm not much of a grown-up. I go out to lunch a free woman, and come back adopted by a child.'

Ha-di-da birds forming a raucous chorus from trees in her shady Johannesburg garden, Sue and I laugh a lot and I enjoy the atmosphere in the lively area of Parkhurst, where she lives.

My presence in Jo'burg is for something else, a school reunion, and it is by lucky chance I find out Sue lives here. Having played with ideas of each other for decades, the reality between us is warm and easy and it is Sue who suggests a visit to Soweto.

Chapter Two

MEETING FREEDOM

Freedom

Soweto, September 2003

The deaths of children who were bright enough to join with thousands of others to protest about conditions in their schools are honoured too, in a church called Regina Mundi.

The large, brick building gave shelter to people fleeing from the bullets and tanks in 1976 and in the bloody years which followed. It is famous in South Africa, not just for the safety it provided then, but for the courage its clergy displayed in the years until Mandela's release in 1990 and the beginning of the end of apartheid. Priests harbouring those fleeing from the security forces were themselves threatened with torture and death for keeping faith with their congregation.

This history is stored in a church big enough to hold a thousand, empty at the moment, light streaming in through large windows onto long rows of vacant seats. Jabu, a friend of Sue's and our guide for the day, takes us to a small dusty foyer to show us the unrepaired bullet holes in the ceiling.

Emerging into the sunlight, I turn round and go straight back inside. There is something about the simplicity of the building, the plainness of its walls and rows of empty chairs, which demands more time and attention.

Tucked away, out of the main body of the church, near the bottom of a stairwell and beneath the bullet marks is a small plaque dedicated to the Youth of '76 who 'pierced the darkness and desolation with their hope'. Copying these words into a small scrunched-up notebook, always carried with me, it is the second reference seen to the Uprising and the date, 1976.

Back outside, Jabu is ready to drive us on. As a professional guide who lives in Soweto and knows it well, he is used to showing people round, but I am not the best of tourists. Asking him to stop every now and then, I need Sue and I to be out on the street among life as I remember it. With Sue game for this, we sit on a pavement sipping cool drink from a bottle, watching life go by. A memory from childhood, sitting like this, no faces to be seen from here, just an endless procession of legs and feet, all of them going places, all of them different.

Moving on to the place where words are written on a boulder, the official memorial to the children's deaths is a new building and its quiet precincts, the Hector Pieterson Museum.

Inside, some of the leaders and survivors of '76 are captured on hand-held camera footage transmitted from small TV screens mounted on the walls, folding brackets behind seeming like a line of stick insects.

The events of the Uprising unfold, too, in media coverage of the time, newsreel films from the UK, US, from the South African Broadcasting Corporation through the voices of Nelson Mandela, Steve Biko, and British reporters like Michael Buerk. Photographs of the March depict banners caught in life-sized grainy pictures. 'Africans are not Dustbins' some of them say.

In one sense the story behind the banners can be simply told. Black children learn in 1976 that Afrikaans is to be a compulsory medium of instruction for half of school subjects. Yet this is the language of the regime which oppresses them.

In Soweto, a township with the largest number of schools, pupils decide to organise a march of protest which, unknown to them, will become a key event in South African history: as the boulder outside describes it, 'a turning point'. For on June 16th the police open fire on the March, killing children and causing international outrage.

It will be long years before Mandela's release from jail but, world condemnation aroused, this rebellion by schoolchildren is seen as paving the way for the beginning of the end of apartheid.

Over the next few weeks the Soweto protest spread to other townships and throughout the country down to the Cape. Students were hounded by police seeking to root out the ringleaders and by September of that year thousands of young people had fled South Africa. Those who stayed faced torture and jail sentences, people like Murphy Morobe and Seth Mazibuko who, along with other leaders, were put on trial for sedition.

Wandering around, we see there are words on long glass panels, red on white, white on smoky grey, *red* on smoky grey and, outside in a secluded courtyard, the names of the dead are written on scattered half-size bricks strewn among the gravel: Morris Mashinini, Jacob Nkosi, Johanna Nyati. Sparingly along the walls are the children's own accounts.

Reading my way along, I learn about platooning, how classroom size in the seventies meant children were not only two or three to a desk, but did shifts in classrooms, one platoon of 60 making way for the next an hour later. Taking out my notebook again, I jot down a couple of details, the exact date, June 16th 1976 and something which seems not quite to fit in, about a sniper and a green car.

Sensing my need, my absorption, Sue lets me wander alone. As I walk down a wooden slope into the long-windowed church-height of the foyer, she is waiting. Out into the sun again, more words on stone telling us that this memorial site is 'To Honour the Youth who gave their lives in the struggle for freedom'.

Driving on, Jabu is keen to show us the big changes in parts of Soweto, while in others, it seems, there are none. A town of vast contrasts, it has million-dollar housing in Dube with its 'High bugs' and 'situations' (people with good jobs) and, not far off, miles of roadside shanty dwellings. A town the size of Paris, Soweto has around three million inhabitants and, as one of the once poorest places on earth, two Nobel prizewinners on one street, Nelson Mandela and Archbishop Tutu. Jabu a powerhouse of facts, figures, dates, I take in what I can.

Lunch at Wandies is next, a famous place for eating, drinking and music, trumpeter Hugh Masekela and Miriam Makeba sometimes dropping by and, until recently, Mandela himself. There is pleasure in so much of this day. Eating outside, sun filtering through the raffia, shadows on the table and, like a memory tight in a small fist, all of it, the detail, the oilcloth table-covering, the bougainvillaea, the soft and clear background sounds is sharply recalled.

After Regina Mundi, the Museum, Mandela's old house nearby, the place where Desmond Tutu and his wife Leah still live down the road, and lunch at Wandies, we have one last call.

A place I shall come to know the name of well, a shanty town calling itself the Motsoaledi Informal Settlement, it is Soweto as I remember it from the black and white news reports on TV. Dust, flimsy shacks of wood and corrugated sheeting, no electricity, few prospects. Poverty.

Most of the low dwellings are one-roomed and clustered together in small earth compounds or yards surrounded by fenceposts and wire. Many are metal shades of grey tin and weathered brown and others are painted, one in pink with a blue window frame. While most have windows, some do not.

Each yard faces a wide dirt track with its communal water tap for around 150 people. The track about 200–300 yards from top to bottom, the tap roughly in the middle, it is a long way for people to carry water from either end.

But here a tourist project has begun where local people with a good knowledge of English show visitors round the homes of families who have agreed to allow us in. Those who feel able to do this get paid a little themselves, the tourist guides give a little to the community council, and so the money goes round.

As do the greetings, the talk and the never-far-away laughter. People are as eager to learn of our lives and our families as we are of theirs. Their adoption of the polite-sounding phrase 'informal settlement' is a sign of this exchange, 'shanty town' sounding scary they think, to Western ears.

In this part of Soweto, with around 1,000 inhabitants, there are earth floors, and the yellow telephone boxes I see are the public toilets. Paid for from community funds and from donations, there is roughly one for every 100 people.

Early in our arrival standing in a clearing, looking about me and trying to get my bearings, I find I have company.

I cannot say he approached me for I did not see him approach. The warm air and dusty ground by my side are empty one minute and taken the next, by a slight child who I think from his thin arms and legs is around nine years old.

Wearing a light shirt, sleeveless khaki pullover on top and similar-coloured shorts, his clothes look clean and pressed in this, one of the poorest parts of this township. We engage easily, immediately, in conversation, spoken in deliberately slowed down English.

His name, he tells me, is Freedom. Said with conviction, for such a small child, and with a big OM at the end, like the sound of 'from', not 'um'. 'My name is FreeDOM.' He splits up syllables and sounds and seems grave, therefore, when he speaks, the emphasis on the end of the word. My name he repeats a few times as CaROL and the place I live as LonDON.

I have met hundreds of African children over the years, mainly in East Africa, when little more than a child myself in Tanzania. The meeting with this child is different. For a start, he is by himself. Usually children are in groups. I am struck, as well, by a sadness in him, something weighty he carries far beyond his years. I am taken by what I can only call his fineness, a quality of slight restraint, a way of standing back a little, even though it is he who approached me. And I am struck too, by his dignity.

By the time we have spoken slowly together for a while, looking at each other's faces, stopping, standing silent too, we are already at ease with each other. As Sue and I go in and out of homes, he waits for us and continues our slow talk about where I live, about his school and the fact that he likes English, stories and music.

Freedom is holding a prize possession. An empty old plastic bag, found on a path somewhere and clutched in his hand, it is his schoolbag for the following day and when I ask what he is most looking forward to about going to school his reply is straightforward:

'Having some food.'

When did he last have some food? I ask.

Two days, he replies. Two days ago.

We have chatted on and off for an hour or so. He has waited outside places as I have gone in, been by my side between one visit and the next, has not asked for anything and has been hungry for two days.

Concealing my distress, some older boys are despatched by our local guide to a small shop nearby and, a few other boys milling around now, we wait for their return a short while later with bread, bananas, oranges, apples. When they have all eaten, some apples still left in the bag, they wait to be asked to take more, Freedom holding one up, telling us it is for his brother, before putting it in his pocket.

We have the obligatory photograph taken next. No good at this, I manage to look strangely absent from pictures, as if I am not all there. A version of the old African fear of having your soul stolen, for me it is not having mine put in. But the gathered children like having pictures taken. And thank heavens they do.

Then we are leaving and I have no idea how to say good-bye to Freedom. His seriousness as well as his hunger demand sincerity and what can I sincerely say? I come up with the fact that I have been glad to meet him and am pleased he will be in school tomorrow.

Looking back, the other boys gone, I see Freedom is still in the clearing, bag held in front of him in both hands, standing still, watching us go. My adult head knows you cannot help, feed, every hungry child in the world. My heart, and another part of my head, asks 'why not?' We have the means.

Silent in the back seat, Sue in front, I feel I have betrayed this child. Given him some food, replenishment for a few hours that is all, and then left him for hunger to return. It is my supposedly level-headed cousin who comes up with it. We have known each other only a day or so but, referring to my god-daughter Emma having adopted *me*, Sue turns and says in an even tone:

'I think you've been adopted again.'

Chapter Three

VOICE FROM THE BACK OF THE QUEUE

Iringa school days, Linde and Carol

London, summer 2003

Being in Johannesburg in 2003 comes from a trail of connections going back to my school days in a different part of an African childhood, in Tanganyika. E-mails to begin with, first of all dozens, and then hundreds, all about the same thing, a reunion of people from decades back, from a boarding school in Iringa.

Not Friends Reunited, more urgent than that. An ex-Iringan, Nadia, living in the suburbs of Johannesburg, has a number of crises in the space of a few years: her partner dying from cancer and her own breast cancer which is followed by extensive surgery. Off work and needing to be cheered up, she decides on us, or at least an idea of us as we were then. Iringa a happy time for her, she gets her son Andrew on the job of beginning to track us down.

Iringa was important for me too, the beginning of a long friendship with Linde, now living in Canada, and of learning how to join in and have fun. Too many moves as a child making it difficult for me to find confidence and build relationships, I tended to hang back unless asked to come forward. Two years in Iringa changed this.

The music master, Mr Charles, highly gifted, masses of energy, formed an orchestra and had dozens of us playing, singing, dancing in concerts, sketches, revues. Enjoying music as I did, he helped the extrovert in me to emerge, had me up on stage with the rest. Away from parents, we used our initiative, learned how to be resourceful and to get on.

A motley bunch of around forty nationalities, Greek, German, Indian, Iranian, British, Swedish, Italian, Canadian, French, Australian, there were upwards of 500 of us. Our parents arriving to work in what was then Tanganyika, now Tanzania, they found no schools in most places and only primary schools in others. So, with a catchment area of hundreds of miles, a new secondary school was built, St Michael's and St George's, near the town of Iringa.

A mixed boarding school, roughly equal numbers of girls and boys aged between eleven and sixteen, off we were sent, travelling by small plane, jeep, lorry, bus and car. But where are we all now?

Only half a dozen or so years after the first intake of pupils, most of our parents returned to their original homes, taking us with them. Things changing fast in Africa and with Tanganyika itself moving towards Uhuru, (independence), it was time to step aside.

Starting with a few people she has kept up with and then eventually on the Net, one by one, Nadia locates nearly 100 ex-Iringans around the world. Setting up an 'Iringa our family' website, she has the idea of a big reunion of ex-pupils.

As more people come on line, the weight of e-mails is overwhelming: old photographs, reminiscences, requests for information flying back and forth. Does so and so remember so and so? And where is he and what happened to her and did she marry him, and whatever happened to so and so's father? A trickle on the screen first of all, then a snow-storm and eventually a blitzkrieg.

The site's rules being made up as we go along – and quickly forgotten – waking in the morning, the system takes ages to download, not only multiple spam, but Iringans on the rampage. Overnight, from far-flung corners of the world, over different time zones, and just as if they had never left the dorm, the boarders are busy.

'When were you last a virgin?' growls Nadia, to us all as Mike Ridley sparks into life somewhere in Berkshire letting us know this is his virgin attempt on the Iringa network. And Karen too. Unused to the way the system is set up, she thinks she is sending an e-mail to Trudy and broadcasts her personal angst about fighting flab and a departing husband to the lot of us.

Why should it matter? We ate together, slept in the same dorms, showered together, or at least separately, but in a conga-style relay. The shower placed behind a central marble slab, with an entrance at either side, when your turn came, with split-second timing you hopped in one side, as the previous occupant left by the other. Not a splash wasted, all on the run.

Years later, struggling to write the book of my god-daughter's journey through her illness, I try to put Iringa from mind, but what about the water pipes?

Boys' and girls' Houses stretched in a long line of single-storey buildings, four boys' dorms at the bottom end of the school and four girls' dorms at the top, boys got expelled for being anywhere near the girls' dorms. The other way round, you only got a warning, so it was up to us to do our bit. Large spare water pipes running the length of the Houses were the means. A dusty crawl through the pipes, short shorts, cobwebbed hair, scuffed knees and here we are chaps. All five of us.

No sex at the other end, at least none that anyone is owning up to. There was safety in numbers and if group sex was around at the time, no one told us.

Scandals were few, and, as these things turn out, wrongly attributed. A group of boys got expelled for being in a girls' House, but not for sex, for a dare. Challenged to go for a walk through the junior dorm late at night, this was the point, it was the *junior* dorm they had to walk through, not the senior one where the curvy, enticing, 'peachy' girls lay. A single-file route march along the narrow space separating the ends of the juniors' beds, looking neither to right nor left, and a swift exit at the other end. No harm done.

Until a few weeks later. A sleepy girl turning over at night had seen them tiptoeing by in single file. Her letter home was innocent and unconcerned enough and there being nothing to write home about is probably why she put it in: 'there were some senior boys in our dorm last night, walking on tiptoes'. Her parents' scandalised letter to the Head left him with little choice but to act.

And then the school closed. Numbers dropping from our parents moving us back to the countries we came from, the school would become Mkwawa High School, and eventually part of Dar es Salaam University.

Keeping in touch with Linde over the years where she lives outside Calgary with her husband Don, small gatherings have developed, a few Iringans here and there come to light.

'Coming to the reunion?' she asks from Alberta on one of the regular calls we have made over the last thirty years.

'Not sure. I'm on multi-delete mode with the e-mails. Lost track of what's going on.'

'Us too,' she replies. 'It's been too much, but Don and I are going. So are the Larsens. Why don't you come?'

A few weeks later. 'Okay, then. Count me in.'

But why Johannesburg? is the question many of us ask. Why not Iringa?

No room, Nadia replies. No room at Mkwawa for people

to stay and no room in the town for at least a hundred people. Why not in Tanzania, then? I ask Linde.

Too difficult to organise. Nadia, who is doing it all, lives in Jo'burg.

There is then the question of how to get there. A long flight, eleven hours, it would be good to have company and with around twenty people going from the UK, not difficult to organise you would think. Except we are ex-Iringans, a headstrong lot, unlikely to make civil servants, climb the corporate ladder, or get in a plane together. After even more e-mails and phonecalls, at last I manage it, arrange to travel with a small group including Alan Clube, Clubey, one of our Maths teachers.

So Nadia has done it, found, badgered, and rounded up us ex-boarders from places like Australia, Canada, France, Scotland, Cyprus, Nepal. Most of us are flying thousands of miles at her behest for what amounts to a three-day reunion in a small safari park near Nadia's home, to be with people most of whom we have not seen for decades. Somehow she has got us signed up, paid up and ready to leave. Her last instruction: Get on the planes. BE THERE.

For me, flying to Johannesburg is startling in itself. Not a place I have ever wanted to visit. Once branded Number One Crime City of the World with a history of mining, dust and oppression.

Tickets taken care of, travelling twenty-four hours ahead of the main party, which, as it turns out, is just as well, I get back to work. Ten days to go, head down – and a change of plan.

Chapter Four

REUNION

Poolside drink at Heia

A phonecall does it, makes me change direction when all is settled and spend my first day in South Africa not with fellow travellers, but with my cousin Sue.

'Do you know she lives in Jo'burg?' my father asks on the phone shortly before I leave.

I thought Sue lived in Cape Town.

No, he is sure it is Jo'burg. He will find a phone number for me.

Has she forgiven me our childhood wedding pictures? I wonder, when she was always the bridegroom and me the bride? Taken in the garden of Ncema Dam, some ninety miles south-east of Bulawayo, the small black and white Box Brownie squares are all similar. Dogs lolling in the foreground, Sue and me a pair of distant figures on the lawn, me, bride-like, with a shawl over my head, Sue in a pair of my father's old trousers.

On the phone she is warm and welcoming these years on, insists I come and spend my first twenty-four hours back on African soil with her and within minutes of meeting at the airport, I feel we are friends. She gives me time to be back again, years rolling away, red earth, miles of sky, soft air on skin. Africa: in all the times I was moved as a child, my strongest impression of sight, smell, touch, sound.

I am surprised, though, when Sue says she and her husband Lennart are taking me to the theatre later on. A heavy three-day session with the Iringans beginning tomorrow and little sleep on the flight the night before, I think I will be dropping with tiredness. But *African Footprints*, a larger-than-life musical, has great vocals, terrific dancing and us in the front row.

How does Sue know I love dancing? I do not ask, for on either side of me, there they are, the pair of them, her and Lennart, not a still muscle between them, gently bopping in their seats. Only a few days before my trip to Soweto and meeting Freedom for the first time, I am already at home.

By the end of the show, boogieing in the aisle, my responsible head-of-an-international-charity, mother-of-three cousin, her hard-working husband and me, performers leaping off the stage to join us, 'Do we have to go home tonight?' I call from the middle of the throng.

Cool drink and cake at a nearby cafe, enjoying the ease in

WATERFORD

No. 0038322 61

people's eyes and my sense of belonging, strangers stop to say hello as if they can tell I am someone with a history in these parts finding my way back. The touch of hands again. African handshakes not a shake. Instead, your hand held till, at some stage during the conversation, it is given or taken back.

The setting for the reunion the following day, Heia Safari Lodge where Sue drops me off, is homely, un-posh, old Africa. Comfortable armchairs, old African bar, fan going, fridge rattling, wood surrounds.

Scattered in the grounds our accommodation, a few dozen rondavels, small round buildings with thick white stone walls and high thatched roofs. Beautiful inside, curved walls bringing a sense of peace and seclusion and the verandah an open aspect on the world.

From here I can see lush grass nearby, small creatures and birds, hills not far off, wildebeest, antelope, up on the ridge. Animals within the grounds too, zebra, gazelle, giraffe, the big ones, rhino, buffalo, outside the perimeter fence in the main gamepark next door.

Living most of my time in the bush as a teenager, animals all round, a friend, Thelma, and I spent hours among them. Elephant mainly, large herds, hundreds at a time passing slowly through, spread about the shrubland with its high grass and low trees, their bodies moving silently, only the snapping of branches and, if you were near enough, rumbling stomachs, to tell you they were there. Thelma and I standing among elephant, the herd swaying around us.

'Did you know a woman got kicked by one of these a few days back?' someone behind me at Heia declares as I crouch down next to a zebra.

'She must have been standing at the wrong end,' I muse, only half paying attention as the animal eats salad from my hand. Later I watch one of the staff standing alongside a giraffe and, reaching an arm up, stroke its stomach.

Sharing a rondavel with Linde and Don, there is, from the start, the sound of laughter and voices calling through the trees. Like being back at school again, only this time, as one of the men says, the booze the boys used to distil from rotting fruit and hide beneath the floorboards, is above board. A company of zebra join us for the ritual sundowners we gather for round the pool, taking titbits from the table, dipping in.

One of the giraffes rubs its belly against the side of our rondavel every morning, an early wake-up call for my 6 am walk with Don. The best time. Each morning, crimson, orange, gold, burnished colours of sand, rock, and in the distance, as the sun moves swiftly up, the pink of hills.

Talking about what Iringa did for us, we notice our jobs for a start. Most of us are in public service, teaching, medicine, or in outdoor pursuits, photography, game wardenship, running national parks. 'It's hardly surprising,' Mike Paterson says. 'Iringa was special and we were lucky. It gave us minds of our own.'

After supper by the pool, flickering candlelight, shadows of trees, people sprawled comfortably around in the dark, zebra mingling too, the 'do you remembers?' followed by gales of laughter last well into the night.

Jackie comes all the way from Australia, the freckled, auburn-haired girl who slept in the bed next to mine. Linde on one side of me, Jackie on the other, I woke in the morning to Jackie's left arm swishing over my head as, standing like a soldier, arms flinging out sharply to the side, she did her bust-improving exercises, which have obviously worked.

'Do you mind if I tell people?' I ask her.

'Not if you don't mind me telling them *your* secret.'

'What secret? I didn't have one.'

'Don't you remember. Back to the dorm after lunch and sharing the dewdrops.'

I am baffled, but apparently after lunch was the time when, fetching a small pot from my locker, Jackie and I would rub cream over our shiny, earnest faces to stop wrinkles. That wrinkle worry should have reached into the heart of Africa to strike fear into thirteen-year-olds is, in itself, alarming.

'Well, that didn't work,' we say in unison, starting up another gale of laughter.

Cries of 'You look just the same. I'd have recognised you anywhere' abound and after days of catching up, good food, excellent company and a lot of wine, it ends. Yes, Iringa was special, it happened to all of us and given the odd above or beneath the floorboards bit of moonshine, it was just as most of us remember it.

We had more than our share of tragedies. Linde's best friend, taken by a shark swimming off Dar es Salaam in the school holidays, and her father dying of fever a few years after. And, on the Iringa list, as more names and contacts are built up, it is clear from the RIPs how many of us have died young. The time for parting, then, is not difficult. This is a beginning.

Sue, who has insisted on fetching me from Heia on this Monday morning, will now take me on somewhere else. Much as I would rather spend more time with my newly found cousin, a colleague in London has friends living outside Jo'burg he has not seen for years and has asked me to say hello for him and bring some gifts. Arranging for me to stay with them my last two nights before they take me to the airport for the evening flight back to London on Wednesday, I do not want to disappoint them.

Driving north, the place where the couple live is, first of all, difficult to locate. Lying next to a motorway, it has no address, only a plot number. When we find the house with its outbuildings, they have an air of darkness and neglect.

At the gate there is an entryphone, there are tall fences and keep-out signs. When we get past these, there are more gates, stockades and barriers encircling the entrance to the house. A pack of dogs emerges from here, barking, jumping up. One, a large grey Great Dane, tries to nip my hand and I keep a wary eye on her.

The man who comes out to greet us is grey-faced, thin and stooped, dressed only in baggy shorts, almost falling off. Prematurely aged, with a sunken chest and sun-wrinkled body, he is ill, and also addicted to large quantities of marijuana from way back. His wife, following, seems tense.

Inside the house is dark, black tiles, dark brick, and heavy security bars on all the windows making it even gloomier. An extra-large TV with poor reception flickering in the gloom, adds to a sense of eerie desertion. Well, only a couple of days, I think. I am so full of warmth, that depressing though this is, it will pass.

But Sue, I notice, says something slowly and deliberately to me, as if I might have gone deaf on the drive over: 'Look, if your hosts are too busy to take you to the airport on Wednesday, give me a ring. Don't forget. Or even before then. Remember, you can ring me any time.'

And I do. By later that day, the warmth and ease of Heia has left and in its place, a dread. The plot I am on has layer upon layer of barricades and heavy, tangled chains. The entrance to the house itself cannot be got into or out of except via its gated enclosure: iron rails round a small courtyard where the front door is and where the dogs stay, except when they are loose in the garden. This has another entryphone, in addition to the one on the main gate in the fence which encircles the whole plot.

The small flat for guests where I stay next to the house, has another set of stockades, iron grids on the doors and windows, chains, yards of them, coiled round and round and a key attached for a small lock somewhere at the end, which is difficult to work.

Something else throws me, a monotonous anti-black diatribe from my hosts: 'If you want anything in this country, these days, you have to be black. We've got the wrong colour skin, hey.' On and on.

Then, out on the road later that day, driving along, there is the incident with the oranges. The wife would like a tray of oranges, calls two 'boys' over, as we wait at traffic lights. Two men each with a tray of a few dozen brightly coloured, seemingly perfect oranges run to the car. She looks at the trays of fruit, car window down, uhmming and aahing for a long time. Yet we are at traffic lights, the favourite place, Sue says, for people to be jumped. This concerns me, but something else far more. Keeping the men waiting, the woman turns to me in the back seat, asks for her handbag, takes out a bulky purse bulging with credit cards, notes and coins and starts rummaging. Purse agape, held up towards the men, she riffles through it.

I cannot bear it. So little money outside the car door, so much on display inside, the men's humiliation. A shrug from her is followed by a dismissive 'I don't have enough change' and off we go. Angered by this, but seeing no point in intervening, I am silent in the back seat.

Back at the plot, the dogs leap again, the large Great Dane bolder this time and definitely nipping. I turn to the woman: 'Please would you keep them in check.'

Given how I am feeling, I probably ask too abruptly, for she is sniffy. 'They don't do it with anyone else,' she tells me.

My one aim now is to stay unbitten overnight and ring Sue in the morning, but getting locked out follows. Walking outside in the garden area at dusk, my bag, keys and belongings are still in the main house. I ring the entryphone to go in and pick them up. No reply. Ringing again and again over ten, fifteen, twenty minutes, I still get no answer. The dogs getting wilder, my heart is beginning to pound. Night having fallen swiftly, I am outside in blackness, the Great Dane a shape nearby nipping at my fingers and then leaping for my ears.

Panic sets in. I am somewhere I do not know the name of, and if I ever get out of here I will never do this again – get taken somewhere without knowing where I am. Even if I could call for help, there is no street address for this place. I only know I am on a plot of land, no lights or neighbouring houses, just the roar of the motorway nearby and rough land all round.

At last a light goes on inside the house and pressing the entryphone again, I am let in. He had crashed out for an hour. She too. I immediately ring Sue. Picking me up at six the following morning, which will have meant a 4.30 start for her, Sue's calmness and warmth melt the unpleasantness of the day before. Little said between us, I do not want to talk about this bleak episode, and no need to, for Sue had spotted the signs: the strange man, tense wife, wild dogs, bad surroundings. Picking up the drug problem quicker than me, she was unhappy about where she had left me and not surprised therefore to get my call.

With my flight not leaving till tomorrow evening, we now have extra time together. She has re-scheduled her work for today and what would I like to do? How about a visit to a township? Yes? Not on my itinerary when I set off from Heathrow a few days ago, not even in my mind, so it is that at 8.30 a man called Jabu picks us up to take me on that first visit to Soweto.

Chapter Five

AN IDEA FORMING

Andile and Freedom

London, October 2003

Returning to London from South Africa, I am haunted by Freedom. Sue had told me how she and Lennart support a family in South Africa, paying for basic food and schooling. She said they both enjoyed visiting the family every few months to see how they were getting on.

Staying with Sue my last night before flying back to London, sleeping on the idea first, I ask her in the morning if I could do the same for Freedom. He has not left my mind, seems to be standing in it still, a picture of a child in the middle of a dusty clearing clasping an empty plastic bag.

Seeing how intent I am, Sue warns: 'Look, these things take time and investigation. If the father's a drunk, if the family's in chaos, we can't do it. It's a hard fact, we have to assist people who can use the help.'

I know this is right and reluctantly leave it there.

The picture Sue sends a few weeks later shows in the background barbed wire, loose posts, a rusting car and Africa's ubiquitous red earth. In the foreground, four boys hold apples up for the camera. Freedom, an apple for his brother in his pocket, is standing both hands holding onto his plastic bag.

There is another haunting in the weeks following my return, the Uprising. Words on the boulder outside Hector Pieterson say the protest was about language, about Afrikaans being introduced into schools, but what led up to this? What was so compelling about this event that years after the killing of adult protesters at Sharpeville, and decades of tyranny, torture and death, schoolchildren should provoke the downfall of a regime where so many others had faltered?

My own brief brush with apartheid was sufficient to glimpse its force and contempt. Seeing black people flinch from the insult 'kaffir' which a Boer neighbour struck at them like a whip, I wanted to be able to stop him. Instead, as a nine-year-old, I was mute.

The class of '76 spoke. How did they do it?

Determined to find out what I can, enquiries in the UK produce the names of two out-of-print books. As I wait for them to be traced, there is little else to go on about what happened to the class of '76 after that year.

Newspaper archives produce headlines of the event itself, including ones from the *Daily Mirror*, Friday June 18th 1976. A big, bold headline SHANTY TOWN CALLED HATE and, underneath, also in large letters FESTERING SORE OF A GHETTO and an opening paragraph:

A million blacks live in Soweto, the South African township which has flared into bloody revolt.

Inside the body of the article, something more human, details of blacks having to pay for school textbooks, while whites did not, and the Afrikaans issue:

The problem which finally blew the fuse on the powder keg is small on the face of it.

But it was the last straw for the people who are already educationally underprivileged.

The battle of Soweto began by a war of words.

No word from Sue, though, no news of Freedom whom she said she would trace through the photograph. Knowing how busy she is, I do not like to bother her, but a hungry child is hungry *now* and this disturbs me. It will take many months to find Freedom through the one snapshot we have and for Africa to take its own slow time.

Thinking it okay to nudge her with an e-mail in early

January 2004, I get a reply saying she had spoken to Jabu just before Christmas and given him the photo of Freedom.

```
Sent:      08 January 2004 11:04
Subject:   Any news?


Jabu spoke to the youngster a few weeks
back and met him and his father this past
Monday. Father does not speak very good
English. Jabu suggests that he makes a
time for me to meet with Freedom and the
father. He will bring them here and then
I can discuss your offer further with them.
I would like to get a bit more detail
about the family circumstances.
```

There is also the news that she and Lennart will be moving from their home in Jo'burg in a few months' time to live by the coast, near Durban. No more from her until May.

I have almost given up, but at last, forty-eight hours before the launch of the book of Emma, my god-daughter's story, an e-mail. The slightly out-of-focus picture of our small group in the clearing that day, Jabu's on-the-ground contacts and Sue's guiding hand have worked.

```
Sent:      04 May 2004 10:32
Subject:   Freedom!
```

Hello Carol,

At long last I have been to Soweto to see Freedom and as you will see from the attachments I took photos of him with his father and brother, Andile. It is interesting that he has chosen to use the English version of his name, Freedom. That tells us something.

I have done a bit of investigating with the school and it seems that these 2 brothers are inseparable, they are both promising students and the head master tells me that they are one of the poorest families at the school, which has 610 pupils all from poor and often abusive backgrounds.

The school tries to provide one cooked meal a day for all the children and this is probably the only meal 'our' 2 boys get. The school has to raise its own funds for the feeding scheme and that is not easy. Their father earns R400 a month [£36] as a petrol station attendant. As you can see they have little in the way of clothing and our winter is just about here.

It is going to be difficult to assist only Freedom as his plight affects his brother and father. By assisting both boys

with a little money to the father so that
he can at least feed these children you
will be assuring there is a structure for
Freedom to thrive and reach his potential.

Carol, I am not too sure how much you
are considering to assist, so I have tried
to give you the details/costs of the various components. The exchange rate at the
moment is R12 to the pound, so for £45
a month you would be making a major
difference in a young boy's life.

I can facilitate any transactions this
end which means we do not lose on bank
charges, transfer fees etc.

Lotsa Love,
Sue

The e-mail also gives me the family's surname, Takashana,
Freedom's African name in Xhosa, Nkululeko, or Inkululeko
as it is spelt in the third person, and his birth date. He was
twelve on 2nd April. His brother, Andile, handsome and much
stronger-looking, is nearly two years older.

Sent: 04 May 2004 14:06
Subject: Re. Freedom!

Dear Sue,
What a joy to hear from you. A big

thankyou for all the work you have done. I know how time-consuming these things are. Please commit me to £45 a month, which I shall set up as soon as I have got round the technical problems of the attachment you sent me refusing to open on screen.

Please begin asap to give the family support (and I will catch up money with you in a few days).

Sent: 04 May 2004 16:29
Subject: Second message from Carol

Dear Sue,

Have re-read your e-mail and picked up that winter is arriving with you. If it were possible to give the family £45 immediately for some shoes or whatever, I shall pay you back when we get the money sorted and the standing order set up. This is lovely news to have.

Much love,

Carol.

The news that Freedom, Andile and their father, Isaac, will have money for food, is like a weight off me I did not know I was carrying and, free of it, the idea of writing something, scarcely recognised to begin with, starts slowly to form.

Twice in my notebook and seen in other places as I have searched for material on the Uprising and its aftermath, there is the date June 16th 1976. It is now May 2004, so the thirtieth anniversary of the Soweto March will be in 2006. Although seldom understood at the time of writing, I have learned to trust my notebook jottings and the dates June 16th 1976 and 2006 are now lodged in my mind.

Sitting on my desk by this time is a book on South Africa's Truth and Reconciliation Commission, Alex Boraine's *A Country Unmasked*. With me because of Sue's account of her work for the Commission, I had wanted to know more. Sitting in her Jo'burg garden, she had talked of setting up counselling systems for the myriad people from all walks of life who gave evidence.

Travelling long distances, uncertain what to expect, some came with hope that at last this dreadful thing could be spoken of. Some, however, were traumatised. They came in hope of finding news, of being told where the bones were buried but were left with nothing. No truth to be found. For others, the breaking of silence was not a catharsis, but a river which would not stop flooding and which seemed to have no end. Hearing Sue talk about the layers of wounds behind the wounds and the layers of healing needed even to begin to address them, Boraine's book is a behind-the-scenes account of the Commission itself and the many obstacles placed in its way.

Appointed its Deputy Chairperson in 1995, he writes of the resistance, the political machinations, the heartbreak, the close calls, the mistakes that went into it and the long years it took from inception to five volumes of witness accounts and findings.

Reading *A Country Unmasked* and excerpts from Commission transcripts, I find myself picking out evidence about the torture of children by the apartheid regime. This happened frequently and, as I will come to learn, included students in the class of '76.

Thus immersed, beginning to talk to friends and colleagues about South Africa, I find people with African links emerge, there all the time, but hidden, waiting to be revealed.

There is Jenny, first of all, a writer and editor. Within days of asking her what *she* knows about June 1976, she takes me to a South African book reading. On a hot, hot Saturday afternoon in central London, the occasion produces Paddy, who is also South African, and who, it turns out, lives with Liz less than 100 yards away from me as the crow flies. We have not met before, but we could stick our heads out the window and call each other over.

A journalist, photographer and raconteur, he talks about being a *white* student in Jo'burg at the time. Police harassment, along with vibrant music and theatre and, as he describes it, mixed-race culture and energy, made it the most tense and dramatic of times:

'The system was pretty hard-arsed and horrendous and important things went missing. I'm horrified by the lack of photographic evidence of that time. They raided newspaper offices, burning pictures and negatives. A reduced history is a terrible crime to inflict on the next generation.

'TV had started in SA the year before, I think. But a lot of stuff couldn't be published because of restrictive press laws and there was little documentation left. Mostly the *Rand Daily Mail*, the main liberal paper.'

Perhaps because of this, Paddy is an avid collector and keeper of material about South Africa and within a few days, armfuls of books, documents, photographs, packages, are removed from his ceiling-high shelves and placed at one end of my large kitchen table. He, like others, will urge me to write this story, to redress the loss of material, the burning of evidence.

And, almost immediately, I discover a link. In a book called *Soweto*, with photographs by award-winning photographer Peter Magubane, a black and white grainy picture fits with a fragment in my notebook from the previous September.

The item from the Hector Pieterson Museum had bothered me. Reading words from the walls, a mysterious detail about a green car had made me go back and check, look at it again. Called simply that, 'the green car', as if everyone would know what it was, the few words about it, written by a girl of fourteen, say this car with a sniper inside was shadowing children on two precise dates, the 17th and 18th of June 1976. There was no mention of the vehicle, a green Chev, and its occupant anywhere else.

Leafing through Peter Magubane's book, it is here. Taken from behind, the photograph shows a saloon vehicle, with full registration number caught on camera, being driven along an almost deserted street.

You see the backs of two heads in the front seat, with the

driver on the right, shoulders in view above the seatback, his right arm, from the elbow down, sticking out of the vehicle. An inch or two of shirt cuff showing above the wrist, the arm is held straight, wrist cocked upwards at the end, a small pistol, like a comfortable object in the hand.

A couple of black women in flat shoes standing by the side of the road, absorbed in conversation, are unaware of the peril. A slight drop, half an inch relaxation of a wrist angle, will bring their bodies into the firing line.

Although movement is implied in this image, the picture's stillness is remarkable. No sign of the vehicle's speed, the driver levelling the weapon, nor the women's impending flight. The car accelerating as it drives away, the gunshots, the women, hands raised, fleeing, are all still to come. The caption accompanying the image tells us the car is a green Chevrolet, a police vehicle cruising the streets of Soweto in June 1976.

And so the story of that time begins to unfold, along with my desire to tell it, while Sue's continuing e-mails bring news of Freedom and Andile.

```
Sent:      11 May 2004 10:26
Subject:  School fees, uniforms etc.


Dear Carol,
    I have now paid the school fees for our
2 'little guys' and also deposited money
in the father's account for him to buy
food etc. I have priced basic school
```

```
uniforms and Jabu will assist in taking
the boys to a local store to be fitted.
I bought them a warm fleece top with hood
last week as the cold weather is moving
in.

    Next week on Thurs. the packers will arrive
and then on Friday they will pack every-
thing and move it down to the coast. We
will follow by the end of the month.

    Lotsa love Carol and I shall keep you
updated!
```

Shortly before Sue moves to her new home along the coast from Durban, Paddy comes over with more to add to the columns of material now almost taking over the kitchen table. He has something else too. Going to a funeral the previous week, he had talked to a man he thinks I ought to meet. An editor and journalist imprisoned in South Africa for his anti-apartheid views, Paddy thinks Paul Trewhela will have invaluable material for me.

Ringing Paul to see if he would like to meet, he suggests I visit a woman called Yael first. Proudly on display in her North London home she has a few remaining copies of her late husband Baruch Hirson's book, *Year of Fire, Year of Ash*. One of the out-of-print books about June 16th I am trying to trace, I buy one from her. On the 'hotly banned' list in South Africa in the eighties, it has a bright red cover and becomes my little red bible. A record of events surrounding

the Uprising, its foreword, brimming with energy, speaks of
the courage of the schoolchildren and their extraordinary unity
as, with one voice, they burst through the pages of history.

```
Sent:      17 May 2004 11:46
Subject:  Re. school fees, uniforms etc.
```

Dear Carol,

  I spoke to the headmaster of the school
today. In fact he was in Johannesburg for
a meeting and I asked him to come and see
me as I had 35 years of *National Geographic*
Magazines to donate to the boys' school.
He is a very progressive man with lots of
ideas as to how to improve the lives of
his learners. He has promised to give me
an update of the progress of the boys and
to generally keep in touch.

  I can't wait to get a bit more settled
again. I hate moving.

There then follow a few weeks where Isaac's bank details
don't work. Not used to receiving sums of money, he has got
the account number mixed up with the sort code and his
pin number and confusion ensues.

```
Sent:      05 June 2004 05:46
Subject:  Re. warm greetings from Carol
```

Hi Carol,

Sorry about the delay but we have been trying to get our 'space under the banana palm' sorted out. Today I fly to Taiwan for 10 days of work which in typical Chinese style will be hectic with visits to 24 centres, North, South, East and West of the Island.

We seem to be making progress with Freedom's father's bank details but it is slow, as is much of Africa. Jabu is trying very hard to assist but had his taxi broken into last week so he lost all his contact details etc.

Must dash as I have a plane to catch. I get back on the 16th. Have a meeting in Johannesburg on the 20th. but will be back here on the 21st.

Sent: 23 June 2004 08:30
Subject: Hello Carol!!

Hello Carol,

I am back from a crazy, hectic trip to Taiwan and am now catching up with myself and work.

Well, I am delighted to tell you that at long last I have the correct bank

account details for Freedom's father and
the boys have school uniforms. I shall
try and visit the family again in a couple
of months. I know they are very grateful
for the assistance that you are giving
them.

 Must get some work done. The Indian Ocean
is looking good today, as blue as blue
can be.

Swiftly I put forward a proposal for a book. Like the
stalagmites of material on my kitchen table, the story has
been growing in my mind and however much of it has
been burned, lost or buried, I want to bring this Sowetan
story back to life.

I cannot say exactly what it will be at this stage, I tell
my editor, except that it will honour the Children's Uprising
and also tell the story of a small family in Soweto now.
Although the two narratives are vastly different in weight
and timescale, their connection is important, for Freedom
was hungry when I met him, as children were thirty years
ago. What has been achieved since then? What is the legacy
of 1976 for black schoolchildren now? And, importantly,
what can be learned by the rest of us from what they
did?

The book's title, at least, is already here, *A Child Called
Freedom*.

Sent: 30 June 2004 07:58
Subject: Re: from Carol

Dear Sue,

The proposal for the book I phoned you about is being considered by the publisher. I have no idea yet whether it will be accepted. To meet the 30th anniversary of the Uprising, I would have to deliver a manuscript by summer next year. Not much time, but a chance to come to Africa again, to see you and Len, to make sure the Indian Ocean is as blue as you say.

Chapter Six

ASKING FOR MORE

School lunch, 2004

The apartheid regime overlooked Dickens in its banning orders and censorship laws and, crucially, it forgot about *Oliver Twist*. It did not stop to think what effect this story might have on young hungry South African minds eager to be fed. Township teenagers crowded together, both in and out of school, devoured the story of this poor English boy.

For them it was a revelation. Systemised oppression of children was happening in England too! They were not alone then. Workhouse conditions, random beatings, slave-labour, cruel taunts, and gruel-like rations were part of a child's life in the world outside as well.

The book was not like a story from somewhere else, nor from a hundred or more years before. It seemed to describe their lives now and it gave them heart that a distinguished author should provide evidence of their plight.

Dickens's novels, *David Copperfield*, *Bleak House*, *Hard Times*, *Nicholas Nickleby*, were read, mainly by candlelight, *Oliver Twist* a big favourite. An ex-pupil in his forties, speaking on the phone, describes reading it in a group:

'Four or five of us would be together and discuss the story. And his books were not banned! Imagine that. We were so happy to read them. The authorities didn't know what was in these books, how they helped us to be strong, to think we were not forgotten.'

Which is how the story of this fictional English boy, 'real' because familiar, formed part of a fightback against the system called Bantu or 'native' Education as it was sometimes called, which gave black children a deliberately inferior system of schooling to whites.

Resistance to it became widespread and with *Oliver Twist* in mind, one of the leading colleges in the country, Lovedale, Cape Province, found its highly articulate students had formed a committee – to ask for more. Calling it The Board, a pun on Dickens's Board of Guardians, they asked for more meat, more lessons, and more and better books.

With a black child's schooling, at one stage, receiving only 5 per cent of what was spent on a white child, this did not seem too much to ask for. The inequities were obvious, but the request had dire results.

The one thing worse than being subjected to Bantu Education was being expelled from it. Students excluded from one school or college were permanently barred from any other, their education and 'the chance of growing your mind', as one parent put it, stopped. And although joined by their parents in protesting at Lovedale, 152 students were charged with public violence, some were detained in jail, and all were expelled, banned from the system.

In another incident, in the fifties, a school servant accidentally got the cups of black and white teachers mixed up in the strictly segregated staffroom. After a white teacher hit the servant, word got round and pupils took action. Removing the white teachers' chairs and hiding them before Assembly the following morning, they left black teachers' chairs still in place.

This was a rare occasion when black people sat while their white colleagues, not prepared to cross a racial boundary, stood across the aisle. This too was heavily punished. The police were called, a number of students arrested and twenty alleged ringleaders expelled.

By mid-July 2004, with a go-ahead from the publishers, I am immersed in this story, the surfaces of my home taken over by papers and documents, and the chairs by people with stories to tell. Making arrangements to see them, contacting people in the UK and in townships in South Africa, searching out poets, trade union leaders, teachers, writers, journalists, academics, the story is emerging.

As well as Dickens, the schoolchildren and students of

the time had other powerful and influential allies. To counter school exclusions, to try and make up for the many deprivations of Bantu Education, including the fact that it was not free and there were children who had no schooling at all, organisations were set up in the community.

Archbishop Trevor Huddleston was asked to form a committee to find alternative places for children to gather and learn. Later transformed into the AEM (African Education Movement), his was one of many organisations where township children were helped with reading, music, drama and games.

Poetry recitals, jazz sessions and just having a place to go, were all part of a tapestry of providing as much education as possible. There was also SAD (Society for African Development), set up in Soweto in the sixties, providing debates, group discussions, seminars and out of school activities for children who were either not in school, banned, or not getting what they needed from inferior textbooks and overcrowded classrooms.

This meant that the reading and writing ability of numbers of people in their mid and late teens was remarkable, considering the circumstances. There was such a big appetite to learn. LEARN itself (Let Every African Read Now) and TEACH (Teach Every African Child) were organisations often run by women's groups, or by sympathetic teachers after school in church halls. They, too, were designed to help children get an education and exercise their minds.

But the apartheid regime did not relent. When, in 1958, students at Fort Hare University protesting about the dismissal of black staff members said these sackings made 'the normal pursuit of academic activities almost impossible' they were met by something which thwarted them further. The following year, the mis-named Enlargement of Universities Act reduced considerably the number of black people able to take part in further education.

In the 'official' words, the Acts, the rules, the documents, the re-drafting which preceded and followed, the regime mis-named and re-named many things, including people. One of the many thousands of people who went before the Race Classification Board remembers being instructed to take the pencil test where 'you were made to jump up and down with a pencil in your hair. If it stayed in you were one race. If it fell out, you were another.'

This separated families. Part of a general policy to segregate people tribally into separate Bantustans, or so-called 'homelands', it formed part of the conditions which faced children outside school. And within Bantu Education, there was name-changing too. Black education was initially put in the hands of the Department of Native Affairs. This changed its name to the Department of Bantu Affairs, which changed to the Department of Bantu Administration, for the purpose, it is believed, of making things difficult, of tripping people up. When they went to complain, which they did, they were told they were in, or talking about, the wrong department at the wrong time and that was not its name and they would have to go somewhere else. By which time, they named it themselves – Bantu Administration Department – BAD for short.

And BAD kept on going. Through legislation and in hundreds of tricky rules it managed, then, to make life impossible for the mission schools. Most had to close and with them the chance of free books, reading, music and the joys of being allowed to read and sing, in the company of others. There were further dismissals of black teaching staff, library closures and even further reduction in funding. Things were indeed BAD.

But protests continued. Trade unionists, local elders, churchgoers, women's groups, all fought for black children's right to be educated. Unwittingly, the regime had made fighting for this a unifying force between parent, child and the community.

When the protest in Soweto twenty years later became, as many have said, 'an unstoppable force', this was because tens of thousands of people of many ages had already pushed against the wall. In this they found another formidable and distinguished ally – Shakespeare.

Travelling over in book parcels, he, like Dickens, slipped under the wire and was read avidly. In gatherings of neighbours, cousins, friends, the volume (kept in a plastic bag under the bed and removed with care) was passed round, people mainly between the ages of eleven and twenty taking it in turns to read aloud by candle and moonlight. Communal Shakespeare readings led to animated discussions about morality, philosophy and the link between personal actions and large-scale events.

Macbeth was particularly prized. The anguish, treachery,

the death of innocents, wringing of hands and the toppling in the end of a man grown weary with a life of bloodshed. In homes, and at performances in church and community halls, young people of the townships took this play to heart.

> Fair is foul, and foul is fair . . .
> Is this a dagger which I see before me? . . .
> Out damned spot! . . .
> Bloody instructions, which, being taught, return / To plague the inventor . . .

The play still performed in Soweto, people remember the effect of words like these on their own struggle, the language pleading not revenge, but natural justice. As with *Oliver Twist*, *Macbeth* was seen as a morality play of wrongs eventually righted and it gave black South Africans a sense of being included in a world-wide literature of tremendous human importance.

Young minds devouring words like these, found them rich with possibilities and with recognition of the link between the words, the language on the page, and what was occurring daily in people's lives in the townships. Fathers who were 'kings' of the household had their dignity slain, called 'boy' in the street. And mothers were shamed too.

Shakespeare spoke it one way. *Drum* magazine writer, Bloke Modisane, did it another. Writing of his time as a boy watching his mother being insulted, sworn at, called 'kaffir meid' by young constables and dragged to the kwela-kwela van, he recalls himself being 'hopeless in the coffin of my skin'. Part of a group of fiery, talented *Drum* writers and photographers working in the fifties, he wrote alongside people like Henry Nxumalo, Mr *Drum* himself, who was filing in Jo-burg, dangerous stories from under a black skin.

Gangsters or 'tsotsis' (pronounced 'totsies') aside, the burgeoning young population of Soweto by the mid-seventies had at its disposal enough words to present their arguments eloquently and, in its ranks, hundreds of platoons of teenagers determined to use them. Apartheid with its weight of tanks, arms, detentions, torture, bannings, deportations, slippery language, in the end failed to stop them.

It slaughtered many and in doing so punctured the sense of being relegated to the living dead which black adults felt at that time. Bringing them nightmarishly awake, it broke, too, Premier John Vorster's lie to the world that there was no crisis in South Africa. The March that day, schoolchildren and the regime which kept them down, conscience and the lack of it opposed, produced for the world a different story.

A long chain of events and horrific times would follow. The event, like others, would be hi-jacked by political extremists and hoodlum elements, but on June 16th 1976, thousands of young people with hungry minds and bodies took on the State. They marched for a principle which they were set to deliver in their main vehicle, words.

Armed in this way, clear and determined, their innocence lay in these qualities of clarity and conviction and their belief that they would be allowed to speak. The right to do so was something hundreds of them died for.

Chapter Seven

A LONG STORY

Garden weddings, Carol and Sue

In the summer, Sue surprises me again. E-mailing her to say there is so little emotional information about the Uprising, her response reveals how intensely she feels about it.

Sent: 14 July 2004 13:06
Subject: Re: book from Carol

Hi Carol,
   At the time of the uprising 'authority' ruled and all that most residents of Johannesburg knew of the horrific happen-

ings on their doorstep were clouds on the
distant horizon of black smoke from burning car tyres and vehicles. Remember, the
news was censored and perhaps peoples'
feelings were too.

But the events of that day are so steeped
in emotions. For me it is the most important day in the South African calendar. It
is a day that reminds us all of the baggage
we carry as individuals and as a country.
We can 'hang it' on that day.

Sue as my helper and protector is a role which begins when
we are both nine, shortly after I arrive in Africa for the first
time, stepping off a ship in Cape Town carrying two large dolls.
Almost as big as me, one in either arm, the three of us catch
a photographer's eye and our picture descending the gangplank
is put on the front page of the *Argus* where, unknown to me,
my Uncle Harry, Sue's father, worked as a printer.

Which is how Sue, who had lived in Africa for years, came
to see it and how she and I came to develop an idea of each
other which will remain for decades. But before I meet Sue
on my arrival in Africa that first time, there is a journey out
into the bush. Our new home, up in the hills, miles from
anywhere is a place called Ncema Dam, our cottage one of
only a few houses.

Although the setting is idyllic – lush green lawns; bright
orange, purple, red, yellow flowers; the different scents of a

variety of shades of sweet pea – I am alone in this garden of Eden. No children in the other houses to play with, my father at work and my mother busy trying to adjust to bush living, defending her kitchen against hordes of invading insects, school for me is a lonely affair, in these pre-Iringa days – a correspondence course.

Sitting by myself each morning in our living room I wrote the allocated work sent in thick buff envelopes – dozens of sheets of paper in a package franked with zig-zag lines, not even an interesting stamp. The work is okay for a while, doing maths, reading and writing. But I finish the sheets for the day too quickly and it is then a long time till I am called for lunch. I soon learn not to fill in extra. It leaves me nothing to do by Thursday.

A chameleon as a classmate entertained me, a secret of course, hidden from my mother's watchful, house-proud eye. Walking soundlessly along curtain rails, its half-lizard-like, half-human limbs and swivelling eyes are fascinating and I move it around, watching as it slowly changes colour to match where it is put. Beautifully camouflaged on cushions or curtains, it went unspotted if my mother suddenly appeared and came out for the afternoon hidden in my dress pocket.

Further to pass the time, we grew me a fringe, my waist-long plaited hair sprouting a pelmet in the front. And a dent from where, having been washed and pulled straight to cut, it flicked up again when dry. Home haircut for my mother too, an uppity quiff in the same place as mine, middle of the forehead.

The other pastime to fill the long hours was dressing-up, a trunk of my mother's clothes a treasure trove of dresses, shawls, scarves, high-heels, beads, bracelets, blouses and all kinds of colourful garments she had bought specially to bring with her, thinking we might go out. Decked out in these, pictures taken of me playing with the dogs or looking wistful among flower beds, are captured in the Box Brownie squares stuck in the family album. But it was not enough for a child's growing inquisitive mind.

Adopting baby dik-dik orphaned by our Boer neighbour's hunting bouts by day and reading myself to sleep at night, I eventually took to writing. Not a new activity for me, pencils carried about my person from when I was six or seven, taken up like slender messengers or miniature cudgels against my distress. Getting easily attached to people, my father's job then changing and us all moving on, my path was already strewn with difficult partings and goodbyes.

Notes left in various trees and bushes about the place became part of a 'paper chase'. Inventing a reader for these scribbled messages was my way of coping with separation and loneliness, trying to join up the dots. Sometimes forgetting where I put the notes, or spotting one gone, taken by the wind or moved by an animal, was cause for excitement and anticipation, the fantasy of them being read. It could not go on. My parents waking up at last to my plight, a letter is dispatched.

So it was that my cousin Sue came to stay for half-term a few months after we arrived in Ncema. Her parents, baby brother and she living only four or five hours' journey away, she would keep me *real* company at last.

But unknown to me, my picture on the front page of her father's paper made a deep impression on Sue. It seemed to her I was important and something her parents said about it being sad for me to have to leave my grandparents in Wales put in her mind the idea that I needed to be taken special care of:

'I can remember thinking that my cousin Carol, who had come a long way, had to be looked after, protected.

'And when we met, you had a real sense of sadness about you. It was as if I wasn't meeting the real Carol at all, I was meeting someone who was struggling.

'We had fun, together. I remember us dressing up from that suitcase of clothes and of *course* I had to be the bride-groom. It was confirmation of the fact that I had to take care of you.'

But Sue seemed sad to me as well, unsmiling as she was in most of the photos and, from what I recall, someone who kept herself in reserve. For the idea that she should put me first came from an unwitting feeling of unworthiness from her own home, a sense from her mother she could never do enough to please her. Not deliberate, but with Sue's mother, Joy, a busy, practical woman, involved in committees and sorting out other people, easy to see how it might arise.

And so Sue and I slowly develop and consolidate our early, young ways of being in the world, Sue's to be dutiful, to take care of *her* pain that way, me to write it down. Leading our separate lives over subsequent decades, Sue marrying Lennart and having three children, me going into journalism and then coming home to write books, we live on different continents, Sue returning to South Africa after a spell in Sweden and me settling in the UK. Not hearing from her at my seat behind the typewriter, I think it is because she is busy. She thinks the same about me.

Years later, in her garden, Sue talks about Ncema Dam:

'It was the first real physical contact with another girl my own age and I felt we had a connection of some kind, so I was very sad when you left.

'And from then on I didn't know much about your life. A couple of times over the years when I heard you'd gone to Canada, I thought "Wow, maybe Carol will come to South Africa one day."

'So when you did come it was very special. I was open to whoever Carol might be and it was wonderful that I met the real you at last.'

A clue to the survival of this person, the real 'me', is to be found at Ncema, in people who were not to be seen for the most part. There were black families living at the foot of the hills, people who survived well on vegetables from the gardens, fresh meat in the bush and keeping out of our Boer neighbour's way. Living in Kraals, hidden from view, I found among them something enduring.

Our home surrounded on its outskirts by thick bush, I was warned not to stray, but boredom and the wish for company drove me to roam beyond the garden's tamed edges.

I followed Walter, our gardener, to his home on occasion. There, the women in his family 'oohed and aahed' over me, marvelling at my skin and long fine hair. Making a fuss, their smiling acceptance spoke of kindness and something more, a kind of celebration. The opposite of apartheid, strangers were much welcomed and in Walter's family's eyes, in their long, deep gazes, the world felt friendly and warm.

On another occasion, trailing after Walter to the edge of the hill, I saw this happen in a different way as Walter greeted a long-lost cousin. What I saw in their slow greeting was, again, something in their eyes: re-kindling, family remembrance, an indelible picture.

Different from the swift and sometimes concealing nature of the glances I was used to in my young life of hasty greetings and partings, I came to enjoy these long, deep looks. They are what my time in Africa has come to mean to me, then and now. Solitary, yes, but deep and remembering, like a footprint in my mind.

Chapter Eight

STUNTING MINDS

Boy and Girl at Motsoaledi

Long before the schoolchildren of Soweto took to the streets that winter morning in 1976 there had been bad trouble in schools and colleges throughout South Africa. From decades back, overcrowding, hunger, regular beatings by black as well as white staff and, as one report said, teachers who exercised 'Nazi-like control' over children were the norm.

It was difficult to tell which was worst, 50–60 people to a class, too few chairs, no pencils, or the strange 'tiredness' which children who were eager to learn spoke of.

'They were too dazed to use their minds' is how a black

teacher at the time puts it. 'Their stomachs were empty and their heads couldn't work.'

Yet parents themselves had gone hungry and had worked extra long hours to find the money to pay for this thing called Bantu Education.

Controlled by the Department of Native Affairs, the first of many oddities was its deliberate policy to thwart black children's learning. It was not *for* education, but against it. Stopping – or at least trying to stop – children from developing their minds was an intention publicly announced by Dr Hendrik Verwoerd, Minister of Native Affairs from 1950 and Prime Minister from 1958:

'I will reform it [Bantu Education] so that the Natives will be taught from childhood to realise that equality with Europeans is not for them . . .

'What is the use of teaching the Bantu child mathematics . . . ? There is no place for him above the level of certain forms of labour.'

and

'People who believe in equality are not desirable teachers for Natives.'

With classroom conditions more like detention camps than schools, food was another major cause of concern. A three-tier system provided meat and vegetables every day for teachers, the same once or twice a week for children whose parents paid the full amount, and only maize or mealie for the rest, the children whose parents paid less.

But then, parents who had paid for their children to be

educated discovered these same children were used as free labour to sweep yards, repair roads, dig gardens and crack stones before and after school. One Province fired all its maintenance staff, making boys do the work instead.

As well as hunger, beatings and compulsory hard labour, children had to cope with inferior schoolbooks, and books of all kinds were scarce. One library had nine titles between 600 pupils and, in the mid-sixties, a number of Soweto schools with nearly 2,500 pupils taking science had three microscopes between them.

Sindiwe Magona, a mother of three, now living in New York, came through the Bantu education system, as did her own children. An acclaimed writer, in her book *Forced to Grow* she describes it as: 'the farthest thing from education . . . inferior, degrading. It was not only not good enough, it was poison.'

In her view, nothing in this barbaric arrangement deserved the name of education.

One man, now a teacher, put it like this: 'In the apartheid system a free black child was a wrong thing. They would have said having an idea in your head was illegal if they could have. They were trying to vanish us.'

But despite apartheid's attempt to 'vanish' children and poison their minds, tens of thousands flourished from a young age. For African children had grown up in a paradox. On the one hand they were 'not human enough', as a fifteen-year-old put it, 'to be able to do what white people did'. Yet they were also aware of the injustice of the system which declared this.

Using their minds long before they went to school, ironically, it was not starting school till a late age that gave them a head start. Brought up and educated mainly by grandmothers till they were nine or ten years old, as one man remembers:

'We were taught to be very proud, to have dignity. It was our land that had been stolen. We were told what had happened to our people was wrong. We knew the people who did these things were in a wrong system. We were not anti-white. We were anti the system of apartheid.'

With parents working long hours or living away, and grandmothers the main influence on children's lives, the latter formed, this man recalls, 'a very protective domestic environment' and demanded a strict code of conduct.

'We were raised to say "no" to violence. Institutionalised violence by a race purporting to be superior to ourselves was even more reason why violence for us was a "no-no".'

Grandmothers' proud and traditional upbringing produced something else. Children lived in an outer reality of being ridiculed and degraded and an inner one of being loved and of behaving well. Through this love, and through urging restraint in the face of provocation, grandmothers introduced children to an idea way beyond their years, that of appreciating and accepting difference. The practice of tolerance.

Black children were taught to know the difference between an individual white as a person, and apartheid as a system. They knew and experienced difference under their skin, something Bantu Education could not teach them – or take away.

This was helped by the many whites, including courageous Afrikaners, who stood up and pronounced the system of apartheid wrong. Some of these were Sunday School teachers who taught that *all* human beings were 'God's children', not just white ones.

The mission schools, before they were closed, and Churches too brought in books for the children, offering a varied diet for hungry minds. This would help to make exceptional people of some of the teenagers growing up, women and men with strong consciences and remarkably versatile minds. It engendered, especially in the class of '76, an extraordinary quest for 'right' to be done, and for individual conscience to be followed.

The devotion to conscience is something they carried like a torch for the freedom to be human enough to use their minds. They saw 'real' education as providing them with this, conscience and human-ness coming together, their following of one and yearning for the other producing in them a love of learning, of books and words.

Chapter Nine

REASONS FOR SILENCE

Enjoying a book

London, summer 2004

The March or Uprising happened on a Wednesday, June 16th 1976, yet one long published account calls it a gun battle, as if between two armies, rather than schoolchildren attacked by police, and claims it happened on a Tuesday. In documents, letters, books and in phonecalls too, tracking down leaders who are still alive, the evidence reveals a problem.

'Facts', they slip and slide around the place, as if the words in the stalagmites on my kitchen table re-arrange themselves at night. In different, sometimes impeccable sources there are discrepancies in details like spellings, figures, dates.

Place names are spelled differently I will discover, even on signposts along the road – Tokosa and Thokosa. The Museum I have stood in front of, Hector Pieterson, is spelled Peterson and Petersen and there is poetic licence too.

Taking myself off to a specialist bookshop, talking to its friendly manager, is she aware of this? I ask. Details, big and small, lurch from source to source, book to book. They tilt and the story will not stand up straight.

While a mainly oral tradition accounts for some of it, words changing as they get written down, this is a part of history that was not meant to be told, she says, 'not supposed to be'. Herself born in South Africa, she says the apartheid regime's determination to hide from the world that they had opened fire on schoolchildren resulted in so much spin and counter-spin, it was a time of utter confusion.

She does not know how people in the township kept their sanity, the banning orders, the censorship before and after and the, looting, burning, threats, lies, all too terrible to say.

'People were silenced by it,' she says. 'You'll find that they won't speak about it, even now.'

Preparing for a trip to Soweto in September, contacting people who have overcome the silence, I try and find a path through.

There was a time thirty years ago when millions of adults, exhausted by apartheid, lost the will to fight any more and ten to fifteen thousand teenagers found it for them. One of the twentieth century's heroic moments, one of its most complete and traceable events, it happened, in essence, on one day and was like a starting pistol setting off something from which there would be no return.

And in the years which followed, devastation, a huge price to pay, fourteen years in exile for those who fled, daily mayhem for those who stayed, but a gradual, inexorable, loosening of apartheid's grip, changing the nature of a government, a country. Why won't this story stand up for itself, now, at least?

A TV documentary from September 1976 has as its title, *South Africa – There is no Crisis*, Premier John Vorster's words to the world spoken 'standing atop a pile of corpses', as one newspaper reporter puts it. So, for people who wanted to know, the truth of this event was out by then.

A Thames TV crew, crossing the border through Botswana, going in after June 16th, finds the corpses, hundreds killed, thousands wounded in what it calls 'apartheid's largest massacre of its black people'.

It also finds one of the Uprising's main leaders, Tsietsi Mashinini. Branded by the regime as a machine-gun-wielding agitator, the most wanted man in South Africa, he sits in front of the camera, a slender nineteen-year-old in short-sleeved shirt and maroon woolly hat.

Speaking softly, he describes how he saw a small boy, Hector Pieterson, shot on June 16th, and how, when it happened, a girl stood in front of the child's slight, fallen figure as a policeman aimed at him to finish him off. 'Shoot

for me' she pronounces in Afrikaans, challenging the policeman to kill her instead and, confounded, he turns his gun
somewhere else. But the child on the ground is already
minutes from death.

Tsietsi Mashinini describes seeing an eight-year-old girl
shot from a passing car, her body strafed by bullets. He tells
the TV interviewer that official claims of only a small number
of deaths cannot be true, for he went to the mortuary a few
days later to try and find the girl. The rows of bodies had
numbers on their foreheads and he passed the number 353
before coming across the body of the child he was looking
for, almost unrecognisable from gun wounds.

Asked if he knows the authorities have demonised him,
he says, without rancour, yes, it is the way they do things,
to call him and people like him traitors and terrorists. There
is nothing they can do about it.

The black and white film ends with the sound of wind in
the background blowing across a dusty, barbed-wire-scattered
clearing and a voice telling us Tsietsi fled the country that
night. He never returned alive. Called a brilliant student by
those who knew him, and 'Shakespeare's friend in Africa' by
his classmate and fellow student leader, Murphy Morobe,
his body was brought back to Soweto to be buried in August
1990.

In the leaning and groaning columns of material on my
table there is a just-published book of Tsietsi's life, Lynda
Schuster's work, *A Burning Hunger*. Taking twenty years to
produce, it tells us that although AIDS was the official reason

given for his death, an injury at the base of his skull and one of his eyes gouged out suggest a different story.

Another account involving deaths of the class of '76 is given in a handful of small, plain A5-size journals or magazines called *Searchlight South Africa*, their co-editor, Paul Trewhela, the man Paddy Donnelly told me I must meet.

Paul has kept filing cabinets full of South African information in a corner of *his* kitchen. Original documents, letters, newspapers, out-of-print works are too painful to look at and too precious to give or throw away. Until now, he says, smiling at me over a cup of tea: 'At last someone is prepared to write about what these young people did and what happened to them.'

Paul has had three lives so far: the first as a journalist for the *Rand Daily Mail*, spending almost three years in prison in the sixties for opposing the apartheid regime. Then as a co-editor of *Searchlight SA*, exposing the complicated international picture of what happened following June '76, the stories no one else would tell.

Paul's third life is as a painter and teacher. A painter is what he wanted to be before politics and human rights sidetracked him for long wearying years. Living in Aylesbury, a calm quietly spoken man, he suggests we talk again after I have acquainted myself with some of the material he has sorted out for me to read.

An initial glance is startling enough, suggesting a further sinister reason for people's silence in Soweto. Volume 5 of *Searchlight*, published in July 1990, gives an account of a mutiny and an infamous prison called Quatro, run by the ANC. The ANC banned and underground inside South Africa in '76, but active outside in exile, it helped the class of '76 to flee the country and recruited large numbers of them to fight as guerrillas in Angola. Eight years later these same young people mutinied and faced death in Quatro at the hands of their own side.

I have wanted to know what happened to these fleeing students, especially those less well-known. Tsietsi, one of the most famous, is dead. A few prominent people like Murphy Morobe and Seth Mazibuko, their testimonies of June 16th included in the TRC's findings, are alive and well in South Africa.

Volume 5 tells me that others of the class of '76 ended up imprisoned in Quatro in Northern Angola, tortured by the ANC, the organisation which helped them flee apartheid. This will be verified from other sources and by one extraordinary man who was in Quatro for many years.

An account of the brutality young people faced *within* South Africa is told in a book of short stories, *Call Me Not a Man*, by Sowetan author, Mtutuzeli Matshoba, Mtutu for short. In the foreword he describes the difficulty of growing up in Soweto in the sixties and seventies, the menacing Saracens, being stopped regularly by the police and life in what he calls this 'dog-kennel city'.

He is sixteen years old when the Uprising takes place. Two years later his first story is highly commended by *The Voice* and he is encouraged to continue writing. *Call Me Not a Man* is the result, truth disguised as fiction. Its first story, 'My Friend, the Outcast', depicts a street scene in Soweto one evening.

Police reservists waiting to rob workers coming home on a crowded train with wages in their pockets, they almost kill one man because, his pockets empty, he has nothing to hand over.

Only just able to stop the man being bludgeoned to death, initially holding back for fear of the same being meted out on them, two friends in the story, after the reservists have gone, wonder whether in another country they might be able to be men. Maybe in hell they would be men. But, they ask themselves, are they not in hell now?

Mtutu says he is driven to write because he wants to reflect 'my side of the fence, the black side' . . . 'so that whatever may happen in the future I may not be set down as a "bloodthirsty terrorist".'

About to meet some of the people labelled terrorists by the apartheid regime, a problem with my back brings me down. Stress probably, overwork, my back with a history of storing tension caves in. Unable to sit upright or stand, after crawling for a day, I phone a colleague, Manoli. With a trip to Soweto planned in two months there is no time to lose.

The links between Manoli and me are superficial to begin with. Meeting on a course in London, we spent three years together training to be Alexander Technique teachers. Qualifying at the same time, we know little about each other except that bad backs and pain had driven us to Alexander lessons first of all, and then deciding to train to be teachers of the Technique ourselves.

The average age on the course around thirty-five, Manoli is young to be doing it, in her mid-twenties. She is also young to lose her much-loved mother, returning to Spain on the news of her sudden death early on in the course.

From Manoli's bereavement comes the first real connection between us. She is an avid reader and the desire to navigate her way through the pain of losing her mother turns up the Spanish edition of a book of mine on grief. Passed round her large family of brothers and sisters, read and re-read, she approaches me in the draughty church hall where we do our training to say how much it has meant to her.

I am especially grateful to hear this. The rejection of a recently finished manuscript has dismayed me. Taking two years to write, and digging up material from my own childhood traced through the problem with my spine, later it will be published, but for now its interwoven story of the link between mind and body, past and present, remains buried in a drawer.

Telling Manoli of my dejection over the book's non-acceptance, she lets me know she has every confidence it will find its way. She is sure, she says, in her heavy Spanish accent, she has no doubts. And this is Manoli, sure, certain, all five feet of her.

Hearing good things about her after we qualify, the problem with my back sends me to her, to ask her to be *my* guide this time round. As we work together, Manoli hears of my up-coming trip to Soweto and I of her life-long love of reading, and her young life in Spain.

The youngest of nine, the end of childhood for Manoli happened when she was thirteen and her father threw them out into the street one night, she, her sister who was blind, and their mother. A small-time crook and a drunk, his activities mean they move on a lot and, as happened with me as a child, Manoli, used to waking up in different places, is good at adapting, at least on the surface.

She is also good at taking charge. Although the youngest in the family, it is she, over the next ten years, who will rescue three of her siblings from drugs and alcoholism. And the night she, her sister and their mother are put out to fend for themselves, it is Manoli who finds them a place to stay. Friends just north of Barcelona allow the three of them in for a while and swiftly Manoli becomes the family breadwinner. The friends have a small family business, a sewing factory, and by the age of sixteen Manoli is running it.

Starting at six in the morning, sometimes working till midnight, by the age of twenty she too has a bad back. Operating large industrial machines and carrying heavy bundles of sewing across a long, crowded room cause her tiny frame to suffer.

Having had to leave school, where she would have liked to stay on, a kindly schoolteacher keeps in touch and feeds her agile, hungry mind. He brings her stimulating books to read, fiction, poetry and non-fiction too: history, biography, philosophy, politics. Which is how she comes across her long-lasting affair with Africa, through reading Steve Biko. His love of culture, first hand, impresses her and his wish to preserve black people from the cheap cast-off ideas handed down to them.

Biko's call to link the past to the present is something she relates to, the understanding of connections in order to move forward into the future with knowledge, not prejudice. 'One of the blacks of Spain' is how she describes herself, born in the shadow of a dictator, her grandfather killed fighting Franco.

As Manoli and I meet I tell her of the Soweto book, the woven story of thousands of schoolchildren in 1976, one child called Freedom now, and my own childhood in Africa.

I speak too of the walk-about facts and tilting evidence which will not stay upright and still. I cannot put the story down I tell Manoli, as we work to help my back. I have a hunch I can make it work.

'I know,' she says with a laugh. 'It is here in your spine.'

But I have missed something. I recall Manoli saying she has always wanted to visit Soweto. Asking her why, she says she has wanted to see the place where this event happened, talk to the people there, learn more about their lives. Biko's words were her bible. Reading about black people being 'steeped in fear' and 'operating under a veil of silence' as their voices, their thoughts, almost their existence are denied in the country of their birth, this, she feels, she can identify with:

'Those schoolchildren were very brave, and what they did that day, it did not come from nowhere.'

So, by mid-August, it is decided. An assistant is needed on this trip, a second pair of eyes, ears, hands to help with arrangements, research, phonecalls. I need someone strong, sensitive and observant who will be at home in Africa.

Manoli and I will travel well together.

Chapter Ten

THE TIME BEFORE DEPARTURE

Soweto matchbox houses

Soweto is just over 100 years old. Founded as overspill accommodation for an expanding black community servicing white Johannesburg in the early 1900s, the site which would eventually be given this name was surrounded by sewage farms.

Initially, conditions for blacks in makeshift housing, with no electricity and clean water, meant dysentery was rife. But the population grew to around half a million people and a slum clearance programme, started in the mid-fifties, resulted in more than 20,000 new houses. It also produced a competition to name this sprawling area on Jo'burg's south-west side.

Since Europeans could not pronounce the African names put forward, four years later in April 1963, a solution was found. The *Rand Daily Mail* reported that 'South Africa's largest city within a city' was to be called Soweto, the name coming from the first two letters of the words of its administrative title, SOuth WEstern TOwnship.

Going to Soweto then, or now though, there is a puzzle in the buildings themselves and in their lay-out. Why did a government which oppressed blacks give them detached and semi-detached houses when it would have been cheaper to build in terraces? Why did they allow a lot of ground around these houses and the space for such broad streets? Yes, the buildings were called matchbox houses, set in predictable rows of two, three and four-roomed dwellings: small rooms, with bare concrete floors, as if as one inhabitant said, for animals. But it would still have been less expensive to build in narrow adjacent blocks.

Buried in the documents, a short answer in a specification to the architects: the roads were to be wide enough to allow a tank to make a U-turn. The distance between houses was to deprive people of cover as they moved from one to another. They were to be aligned to give a good firing line. Local people were to be easily picked off.

Something else in these papers, a piece of information to do with police activities on demonstrations. They had a habit of following behind demonstrators, sneaking up, so that if people turned round to run, they were suddenly confronted. It happened that day, June 16th, people at the back ending up on the front line and the whole column of protesters caught in a wedge, police at the front of them and at the rear too.

My kitchen home to even more South Africans bearing gifts, by early September, information overload threatens, the place I usually call a home now a port of call for anyone with a hint of a South African connection passing by.

Paul Trewhela, having spent an hour or two with me a short while back, visits again before Manoli and I leave for Soweto. He has brought more material and adds a weighty contribution from half a dozen carrierbags to the growing clumps of books and papers on my kitchen table. Sitting down for tea and cake, we are shoulder high in South African history.

With an almost photographic eye for detail and dates, and with a concern for justice, Paul has worked behind the scenes to encourage a publicly accountable version of South Africa's recent history.

Born in the country, banished from it because of his anti-apartheid stance, his criticism of the present regime has been as consistent as his fight against apartheid. Like Tebello Motapanyane, a student leader I shall meet in a few weeks' time, Paul believes revealing the truth is vital for a country's health and for the future prospects of its people.

A letter of his on 21 June 1990 to Archbishop Tutu asks for the setting up of what will become the Truth and Reconciliation Commission. One of those small steps on the long road to this remarkable process in South Africa's post-apartheid history, the letter's request is for the *ANC* death squads to be investigated.

It follows a similar request to Nelson Mandela two months earlier from members of the class of '76 who had joined the ANC in exile to fight in Angola and who eventually fled to Nairobi in 1990.

The behind-the-scenes story of this appeal has a terrible symmetry to it. In 1976, young idealistic people rebelled against a system and marched for education. In 1984, on discovering things in the ANC which flouted the democratic structures they held dear, they rebelled again. Only this time, their commanders called their action mutiny and their punishment was Quatro.

The fact that the reasons for this second uprising were as honourable as they were in 1976 would later be proved. For now, shortly after Mandela's release and the moving of prisoners from Quatro into holding camps in Tanzania, a letter dated 14.04.90 is sent to him.

Written from the YMCA in Nairobi, where Archbishop Tutu had arranged for them to be housed after they had fled persecution by the ANC, in essence the letter asks for Mandela to use his influence to reform the organisation they had served and fought for.

Stating that the mutiny was a reaction to corruption in the ANC and to lack of democratic structures within its political wing, the letter describes those at the top of the ANC in exile as 'fake custodians of our people's political aspirations . . .

Calling them 'enemies of democracy' the letter writers protest at these ANC officials being allowed 'to negotiate the centuries-long denied freedoms of our people. What a mockery! What a scorn to our people's sacrifices for freedom!'

Writing that they appreciate Mandela's tireless efforts for a settlement to South Africa's problems, they say: 'We believe that our people's yearnings for justice can only be competently secured by a morally clean leadership . . .

'Hence, our sincere call to you and the fighting masses in South Africa and within the ANC to back our demand for a commission to inquire into these atrocities [at Quatro and in Angola generally]. This, contrary to short-sighted ideas, will not weaken the ANC but will demonstrate to our people and the world the ANC's uncompromising commitment to justice and democracy.'

A copy of this coming into Paul's hands prompts him to write to Archbishop Tutu to ask for a major investigation into what it contains and into similar evidence he and others have received. He suggests an inquiry be set up 'with a major participation of figures with a legal background and an honourable human rights record in SA or internationally'.

Archbishop Tutu's integrity is such that, having lived through the horrors of apartheid and seen countless people suffer and die at its hands, he takes heed of the letters sent to him and presses for an inquiry into *ANC* abuses, along with those of apartheid. Prepared for black South Africa to set its own house in order, he begins the process of persuading others to join in establishing what will become the Truth and Reconciliation Commission.

From this it could be said that the genesis of the Commission goes back to the class of '76, to the letter they sent to Mandela and the information they sent to people like Paul Trewhela. Which is why, for Paul, June 1976 was 'a defining moment' with 'an extraordinary quality of innocence and integrity about it, a remarkable piece of history'.

As for his opinion of why it happened, why so many school-age children would take it upon themselves to organise in this way:

'They were not prepared to take dictation. That's the strength of what it was about, they wanted to think for themselves.'

Gathering his thoughts, his voice breaking, he continues:

'And for this, for their intelligent and humane protest, young people met with great violence from the State. Night after night security forces were in there hounding them – the things we didn't see in the newsreel pictures.

'Only a few years later, they then met with brutality and violence from their own. They were the flowering of a democratic voice in South Africa and the hierarchy of the ANC in exile chose to crush them because of this.

'There was never such a fruitful period of thought and activity as among those young people at that time. They were out on their own.'

On looking through documents, why they were out on their own and why what they did was so extraordinary is to be found in their unique position. For the class of '76 would find themselves in conflict with *both* the giant opposed forces of the mid-twentieth century, the ideologies of Fascism and Stalinism: the former through its influence on the apartheid regime and the latter through its sway over the military wing of the anti-apartheid movement.

Stalin's inflexible dogma-ridden methods having deeply infiltrated the workings of the ANC in exile, those of the youth of '76 who fled the country and chose, afterwards, to join the armed fight against apartheid, found they had fled from one tyrant into the ranks of another.

Innocent of this, of what they would eventually discover of the ANC operating outside South Africa, they were stuck in the middle, wedged, as they had been on June 16th, between one punitive force at the front, another at the back. Out in the open, in the middle of the road, they wanted no part of either the extreme Right or the extreme Left and they were trampled on and killed by both.

News of my research getting round at home and abroad, I find myself speaking to Lynette Naude from her farm outside Jo'burg. Her father-in-law, Beyers, is revered in South Africa as an Afrikaner who had the courage to reject apartheid. A pastor in the Dutch Reformed Church who preached segregation for many years, he suddenly changed his mind in a public manner. Denouncing apartheid from the pulpit he was fired from the Church, put under house arrest and ostracised.

One of a number of remarkable Church people who stood

against apartheid – Canon John Collins, Archbishop Trevor Huddleston and Archbishop Tutu himself among them – elderly now, Beyers Naude is very ill at this stage, but Lynette would still be glad to see me.

Paul Anderson rings from the British High Commission in Pretoria to fix lunch for when I am over. Suggesting Wandies, the restaurant in Soweto I went to with Sue, is that the one Mandela eats in sometimes? he asks.

Yes.

That will be fine.

Linde calls from Canada next. Making our usual monthly phonecalls, she has been delighted to hear of my support for Andile and Freedom. 'What a wonderful way to return to Africa,' she had said. And had added in her usual forthright way: 'You know, some people have a sentimental idea of the past. Us lot [meaning the Iringans] just get on and do things.'

I could do with Linde here. The weight of contact numbers is taxing in this brimful time before departure. Typing out a schedule to travel with, dozens, no hundreds, of numbers for people I will meet jump up to be double and triple-checked. There is a home address and a postal one, too, for some people. And others, as I will discover, travelling between homes in the countryside and the township, give their mothers' cell and landline numbers too.

Photographs, letters, books, names of new people to contact, keep on arriving through the letter box, by hand, by post, by e-mail. And with them, news of the death of Beyers Naude on Tuesday 7th September. His public funeral, one of many services, Lynette tells me when I ring her, will be on the day we arrive, Saturday 18th September.

Arranging to be at Heathrow with plenty of time to spare, Manoli is excited to be going to Africa at last, to Soweto itself, which she has kept in her mind for so long. 'We're on our way!' she says with ill-concealed excitement as we sit in the departures lounge.

We are not. In eight hours' time we will be sitting a few yards away from where we are now, grounded. We will still be sitting at the airport after midnight, and will not travel to South Africa that night at all.

A technical hitch with the plane will have us grabbing a few hours' sleep in a hotel we are eventually taken to and a further technical hitch of some kind will mean we do not arrive until after midnight on Saturday. We will miss the whole of the first day when we had planned to join people thronging the streets for Beyers Naude's funeral procession and to go and visit Freedom.

But for now, at the airport, I am struck by something else. With the momentum of e-mails, numbers, connections, mis-connections, flying in and out of my computer, I have been too busy to notice something.

Sue is not in Jo'burg any more, is living hundreds of miles away on the coast, and not even there for our trip, but away working in the States and Canada. She has arranged for Jabu, a man I have met only once before, to meet us at the airport. He has booked a B&B for us in Soweto. I have no idea where it is or what it is called. I only have a mobile number for Jabu. Nothing else. No back-up e-mail, landline, home or office address. I have no address for Freedom either. Living in a squatter camp, an informal settlement of lean-tos and make-shift housing made of corrugated sheeting and nailed-together walls, he seems not to have one.

Who would set out under these conditions where a flat battery on a mobile or a badly delayed plane could set us back for days? I turn to Manoli:

'Do you realise we're travelling thousands of miles to a place I've been to only once before, to meet a man I've met only once before who will take us to a child with no address?'

Manoli, sitting next to me, turns, looks at me seriously, then away again.

'Mm' she says, nodding her head.

Chapter Eleven

THE WINDING SHEET

Manoli and Neo

Soweto, Sunday 19th September 2004

Neo's is where we stay, off Vilakazi Street in Soweto's Orlando West. The street has a plaque on the corner showing Nelson Mandela and Desmond Tutu hand in hand, two Nobel prizewinners, their houses 200 yards apart. But we have not discovered this yet. It is dark, 1.45 am, and we are glad simply to have arrived after a thirty-two-hour journey.

As we stand at the gate of what was once a four-room house, now converted into a B&B, Neo emerges, woken by Jabu ringing the bell. She is smiling warmly, even at this hour and, after the shortest of hellos, Manoli and I are asleep.

Bird calls wake me first, around six. Different notes, unusual tones and calling patterns letting you know as you come to, that you are somewhere else. Then human voices calling greetings from up the road, down the road, across the way, sound carrying easily. Something I remember from childhood, a clear carrying of voices in the morning, intimate and inviting, making the world outside seem safe.

Padding around Neo's kitchen, dark blue wooden units, soft tiled floor, I gaze longingly outside. I want to sit on the step in the early sun with a cup of coffee, join the early morning ritual of calling out, talking to people, but no coffee to be found. And gated in any case, slender iron strips barring the door. On the other side, broad steps leading down from the verandah, a large inviting bowl of dozens of lemons is also out of reach.

Jabu wanted us to stay somewhere where we would feel at home, he had said the night before. Also, he knew I was working and if people were coming to be interviewed, they could find their way here easily. Mandela's house, the small house where he used to live in Soweto, now a national museum, is just up the road. On the main tourist route, everyone, white or black, foreigner or Sowetan, will be able to find it.

In his mid-thirties, born in Soweto, Jabu runs his own fleet of tourist cars and vans around the township and to surrounding places like Pilanesberg National Park.

On the way from the airport, driving along in the dark, he

had told us about people in the eighties deciding to reverse in there minds the signals of the traffic lights in Soweto, or robots as they are still called. During the years of chaos and bloodshed which followed '76, crime was rampant, including black on black car-jacking. Usually happening at traffic lights, tsotsis stopped your car, took your belongings, threw you out and drove off.

So in Soweto, instead of stopping at red lights where the tsotsis might be waiting, you drove straight through and stopped instead on green. Of course, this sometimes went wrong, Jabu shrugs, and there were a lot of 'misunderstandings'.

What it did, from Sowetans' point of view, was drive the tsotsis into Jo'burg to commit their crimes there, where the whites were caught because they obeyed the robots, stopped on the red and drove off on the green.

The word Neo means 'gift' and, finding me standing at the gated door as she enters the room, Neo opens it to let me out. Within minutes I am where I want to be, sitting on the step with hot coffee in hand, drinking in the morning. Colour gentle at this time of day, grey-pink tinging a hill in the distance, light blue cloth on a kiosk at the corner, soft red earth, grey-green of a large cactus in the corner, and the new fresh green of bushes all round.

Across the road, only a few yards away, is a small primary school and beyond, a view for miles. The low rooflines of mainly single storey buildings and 1950s compulsory tank-turning space, give the eye a clear path through. The feeling of space, then, miles of sky too, light blue, and clear crisp air in this, an early spring day.

Manoli woken by our voices, up now, is as perplexed as I am by the offer of bacon and eggs for breakfast. Fruit we say, surveying the neat cardboard packets of cereals on the table and a regimented row of white bread. Paw-paw, mango, guava, lemons, brown toast. Oh yes, and coffee.

We will spend a lot of time around this table in the next week talking of family, friends and the time of the Uprising. Neo's family, like everyone else's, was affected. Her brother had to flee for his life, and her kitchen with its air of old wood and stillness becomes the place where we talk of these past things.

By the time 1976 was only a few months old, life on the streets and in schools in Soweto was almost impossible. Thousands of young people in South Africa were beaten by the police or security forces, and sometimes killed. Protests over Bantu Education ongoing for decades and Steve Biko's powerful, charismatic presence in the Cape urging black students to be strong, young people's drive, energy and idealism were viewed as threats. They ran counter to a regime determined to keep blacks and coloureds down, and police brutality against youth was widespread.

Not unusual for schoolchildren to be taken to police stations and systematically tortured, they were often detained for weeks without their parents knowing where they were. Tied up, plastic bags put over their heads, they were subjected to electric shocks, made to strip naked, beaten by four or five people at a time, or made to stand for hours on end. Then they were let go, returned to the streets as potential 'sell-outs', the authorities hoping they would inform on their own community.

In this way, apartheid also made children lonely. For knowing this is how the police worked – that they took people as young as thirteen, fourteen and having tortured them, threatened them with even worse if they did not turn informer – they were treated suspiciously after that. Not invited to games, left out of conversations, they were double outcasts.

Those picked up for a few hours and given a bit of a fright were different. One of these, an early leader of the uprising, Tebello Motapanyane, was caught and interrogated for possessing a poem, one of his own. Written in English, it speaks of pain, yearning, hope and a feeling, heading towards dusk, of: 'my mind / coiled with barbed wire'.

That year the wire got tighter.

Afrikaans, the language associated with cruelty, hunger, and being 'un-peopled' as some called it, was to become the means through which they would learn in schools. An edict delivered in 1975 by the Minister for Bantu Affairs announced this: a compulsory switch in some subjects from English to Afrikaans.

No time given to adjust and no official reason given either, the hand of the Broederbond, a group of hard-line Afrikaners, was detected. Anti the English language as well as anti-black and anti-coloured, they wanted South Africa to be Afrikaans-speaking. Many of them Heads and Principals of schools and colleges, they were influential in government thinking.

Besides its oppressive associations, there were other major problems with Afrikaans. Black teachers, having been taught in English, did not know how to teach in it, especially maths and geography, where there were sometimes no corresponding words. Incredulous as well as angered and frustrated, they too protested.

English was a window on the outside world. The conveyor of *Great Expectations* and *Hard Times*, it was the language of commerce and international affairs.

But it was Afrikaans's place in the minds and hearts of pupils which brought about what followed. The apartheid regime had made it not just a stumbling block, but an impenetrable wall. Afrikaans had come to mean something in which black people's personal truth had not been honoured or even observed, in which their humanity had not been spoken and by extrapolation, in which their truth and humanity would not be found.

Having to harden their hearts to the cruelty delivered in it, blocking their ears to its insults, Afrikaans was, as far as the youth were concerned, a dead end through which they could not convey anything real about themselves. Not only would they be unable to learn in this language, but they feared it would rob them of the one precious thing they still had, their identity. A student at the time said:

'We were not going to use Afrikaans. If you let someone take over your mind and identity, that person has dominated you.

'If they imprison your mind, making you something which

you are not, you are done for. We knew if they locked our minds we were lost. We were not going to let this happen.'

The thinking against this identity theft was determined and irrevocable. They would go to the wall for it, tear the bricks down. For all the bad things that had been done to them and for the shadows of people they had seen their parents become, on this issue they would say 'No'.

As if to give immediate support for this stand, in the schools where Afrikaans had been forcibly introduced in January 1976, pupils' marks began to fall. They could not learn. Teachers were in chaos and could not help them. There was nowhere for them to go.

It was for this loss of hope, going back decades, over hundreds of protests throughout the country and thousands of expulsions, that people of school-age in Soweto, mainly between fifteen and twenty-one, organised to take out the bricks in the wall. Resistance to the language that would close them down was well-nigh unanimous and by March 1976 Soweto was volatile.

Police were called first of all to Thomas Mofolo Secondary School where Afrikaans had been introduced and pupils were threatening to burn their books. Word of this spread rapidly through the many community organisations set up to help schoolchildren who wanted to read, learn, debate, act. Through youth clubs, TEACH and LEARN, and through highly attended poetry gatherings where teenagers read their writing out loud, the message was that Afrikaans would be resisted.

Word also spread through SASM (South African Students

Movement). Originally formed in Soweto in the early seventies, it had just about managed to survive as a pupil body. It was this organisation which began sending pupils from school to school as scouts to find out what was going on.

In some schools, with the support of teachers, lessons were suspended in favour of international debate. Information so limited, there were however people who listened to Radio Freedom from Mozambique, who heard the World Service, and who read banned books.

Older pupils like Murphy Morobe and Tsietsi Mashinini, both excellent speakers, were given class time to enlighten others about the state of the world outside South Africa: student unrest in Paris; independence in Ghana from years back, and now in Mozambique. This kind of information was passed round and hungry teenagers picked it up, handing it on in turn from class to class, school to school.

What is extraordinary about these times, from people who are prepared to talk about them, is the students' optimism and orderliness as well as their passion. Among this group of young people there was talk of *orderly* change in South Africa, of the end of apartheid as a long-term move towards enlightenment. It was not revolution in the air, but informed resistance, the need for debate, discussion and education by whatever means they could find. People were elated at the prospect of change at last, and the schools where this was advocated, Naledi High, Morris Isaacson, Orlando West, Orlando High, Diepkloof, were to produce some of the leaders of what would take place in a few months' time.

In this time of flux, after the Afrikaans issue emerged as the catalyst and before the June march was thought of, the township continued to be in turmoil. Ellen Kuzwayo, in her nineties, a highly respected figure in Soweto today and a grandmother even then, describes seeing unmarked police cars in the winter of '76 taking pot shots at people in the townships. One bullet lodged in the skull of an eight-year-old boy sitting on the ground playing marbles with his friends. This shocked her. Used to callousness, the events of that year she nevertheless found deeply disturbing.

In her book *Call Me Woman*, she writes that the police, always claiming to act in self-defence, 'fired at youngsters and left them seriously maimed or, in some cases, stone dead'. She recalls schoolchildren that year as 'exercising commendable patience' in their search for people to take notice of them, to hear their concerns.

These concerns had fallen on deaf ears for decades, even though eloquently expressed as far back as 1958 when students at Fort Hare warned what apartheid policies in education would do:

'We wish to warn the architects of white domination, the whole country and the world at large that we will not be held responsible for the disastrous repercussions, which in the foreseeable future will destroy the entire social, political and economic structure of our country.'

As well as an imposed language and random shootings, tsotsis were ever-present in the township, gangs of teenagers and young men who terrorised people whenever they could.

Even before '76, they kept track of school timetables, swooping in when children were in the playgrounds, forcing them to hand over the small bits of money they had in their pockets. Reports of theft, smashed windows and assault were ignored by the police. Black on black crime suited the regime, adding to the level of chaos, fear and bewilderment that Soweto and other townships suffered.

By May 1976, the level of activity among schoolchildren was high and had formed an energy of its own. Something big was bound to happen as day by day, incidents fuelled passion, excitement and protest. Many teachers and Heads sympathetic, the Afrikaans issue volatile, fervour building word by word, whisper by whisper, class by class, school by school, the March itself, unplanned as yet, was invisibly building.

More than a thousand pupils walked out of lessons at Orlando West Junior School and, at nearby Phefini Junior, the principal's office was stoned for his lack of sympathy to students. Many of the almost exclusively black teaching staffs in Soweto, finding themselves on the children's side, stood by as their charges refused to stay in class.

In another incident in June, police came to collect a student called Innocent from Naledi High. His name belied him for, intercepted by security forces and agreeing to inform on his classmates, all the while he had reported to the latter, running the dangerous path of sending the police off track.

Catching up with him to charge him with subversive

activities, the police came to collect him from school, but the other students were ready. Police having entered the school, they locked them inside the school gates and proceeded to burn the police car standing outside.

On June 13th, a Sunday, SASM called a meeting to discuss what to do. Attended by more than 300 students, it was here the march was organised. The speed was dictated by the knowledge among the few who were politically aware of an imminent meeting between Henry Kissinger and South African premier, John Vorster.

Official American response to apartheid went along with the apartheid government's statement 'There is no crisis in South Africa,' and senior students were determined to show up this lie. As one of them said:

'We wanted to undermine that meeting and show the world our side of the story.'

The Uprising's time had come. Rebellion was growing from within, the bonfire had been ready a long time, only a spark was needed to set it alight.

What people remember most about the event is its intuitive speed and energy, an extraordinary engagement and excitement of being carried along by the determination, and yes, the 'happiness' among pupils that at last they would do something.

Tebello Motapanyane, General Secretary of SASM at that time, chaired the meeting on June 13th where an action committee was formed to organise the event among around fifty-five schools. This would later became SSRC, the Soweto Students Representative Council, and included people like Murphy Morobe, Tsietsi Mashinini and Seth Mazibuko.

There were two full days, that is all, for an event involving thousands of pupils to be organised. But they already knew each other through going from school to school since March. Now scouts attached to each school, voted for by pupils, liaised with the central body and they set to. Travelling daily, exchanging news, the area and its details were already unconsciously mapped. Photographic memories for streets, places, numbers, names, a diagram of where to go, and which route to take, was already in their minds.

Plans were put in place for the precise times each school would start out and the place they would head for to join the main body of the March, placards were made, along with the decision to involve mainly secondary schools. Given the late school starting age, primary children aged between nine and fourteen were thought to be too young to join in. Some sympathetic primary school Heads, informed of an unspecified event in progress, were asked to send their schoolchildren home that day. Parents would not have known, most at work long before children left for school.

But many primary children decided not to be left out of the action, and joined the March, even though they barely knew what it was for. One of them was twelve-year-old Hector Pieterson. The majority of marchers in their mid teens, most of the leaders were older, eighteen to twenty-one.

As for the placards, nearly all of the same mind:

Bantu Education – to hell with it!

Blacks are not dustbins – Afrikaans stinks

Some said 'release the detainees', referring to classmates held in police cells at that time. By 1965, the police could detain for 180 days without trial. A year later, detention was unlimited if authorised by a judge, and by 1976 judicial authorisation had been dropped. Police detention could be unlimited and, there was little way of finding someone who had disappeared.

By Tuesday June 15th when nightfall came shortly after six, they were ready. You would think there must have been rumblings, especially that evening, hints of a slight change in behaviour, the tension of concealment. But parents would have been too tired to notice. Returning home from work after nightfall, they longed for food and a brief respite before the following 4 am start.

People in the world outside South Africa think of what happened next as a headline, the day a town was set alight or the day children rose up and demanded the world's attention. It was not a day. Nor a year. It was an event which had been simmering for decades:

'Like death, the events of 1976 had not hurried, they had bided their time, certain of their mark and sure of their potency.'

The words of author Sindiwe Magona, back from attending a conference in Brussels a couple of months before the Uprising happened:

'On 16 June Soweto burst into flame. We watched in horror as violence spread.'

Describing how, as a teacher, she had seen ideas of freedom growing in young people's hearts corresponding with the
apartheid regime becoming even more vicious and repres-
sive:

'Like chickens in the calm before a whirlwind, South
Africans had worn disquiet for long, weary years. Cooped up
in our pen, we fluttered, beat and bruised our wings . . . we
could not save ourselves.

'Now, hundreds of kilometres away from where I sat, safe
in the knowledge of the vast shielding distance, African children, schoolchildren, left their classes and took to the streets.'

Chapter Twelve

TEBELLO'S STORY

Jabu and Tebello

Soweto, Sunday 19th September 2004

One of the organisers of June 16th, Tebello Motapanyane lives with his wife and five children up the road from Neo's. A phonecall at 10.30 am from someone on the June 16th March produces his address and a short while later, Manoli and I walk up the road to meet him.

Tebello's house is also an original four-room dwelling, but larger than Neo's, added onto at the back to make room for his own, plus a large extended family of brothers, sisters, nieces and nephews. It is relatively bare of furniture, except for a TV screen in one room watched by half a dozen children, and a large kitchen table in the other around which we sit and talk.

Tebello's wife, young and cheerful, greets Manoli and me warmly. Also called Jabu, she explains that it means 'happiness' as a woman's name and 'hope' as a man's. As her husband enters the room, a tall, studious-looking man, wearing glasses, it is clear from the way he moves that he is not well. We had been warned that his sight is a problem. Fading in one eye, he and Jabu are unable to afford the treatment he needs.

Isn't medical care free?

Jabu explains how, yes, you can go to hospital, be seen by a doctor and get a prescription, but sometimes the hospital will not have the treatment you need. Often the pharmacies are poorly stocked. And if you have to pay for it in the chemist, it can cost R300–400 (£27–£36).

If you wait for the hospital to have the medicine, sometimes you wait a long time, which is how Tebello's eye has got this bad they think. Waiting and waiting.

Behind his hospitable exterior, Tebello has other health problems which make life difficult, for in order to claim the child allowance he and Jabu are entitled to, a parent needs to queue for it, sometimes for hours and Tebello faints easily. As their children's mother, Jabu could join the queue instead, but although they have been legally married many years she has not been allowed the relevant documents which would mean she could stand in line for him.

Yet Tebello is not a frail man morally or intellectually, and certainly not cowed, as a two-hour conversation around the table reveals. Glad of my interest in this event, he is keen to discuss it and to link the reason why they marched with problems he sees in South Africa now. When asked to recall June 16th and the lead up to it, he begins by telling Manoli and me what conditions were like in Soweto at that time:

'Most of us young black people had almost the same family backgrounds, hunger, and what the world media preaches about today, poverty. This was our life.

'And when you looked at white people, they had chances, opportunities. We never had opportunities as young black people.'

Discussing the Uprising, which he recalls vividly, I remark that it was still amazing that after decades of poverty, hunger and abuse, thousands of schoolchildren would have the courage and organisational ability to do what they did, to get together and challenge the State.

His response is, initially, surprising.

'We were all extremely exhausted' he says, 'tired of the system. Sometimes we were too hungry to learn at school and everybody was affected at that time, the old and young.

'We saw our parents exhausted by the system. They were good people. They did not believe in violence. But they were traumatised. They were cowed down to a level where they did not want to act or to do anything.'

He describes how the Afrikaans issue acted as a focus as well as a catalyst. It moved them out of their physical and mental tiredness, gave them something clear to talk about and brought about a strange state of expectancy by May of that year, as if something had to happen.

Pupils visiting each other began to form bonds of understanding and determination. Sympathetic teachers, suspending lessons in favour of debating societies, produced another layer of understanding and frustration at what they were all being denied. This was all leading somewhere:

'We were going from school to school, exchanging views with other students and we were beginning to see for ourselves what was happening.

'The whole system was failing us. If you ask him, over there, or her there, they will tell you they want to go to school, but what was holding them back? School fees.

'Our parents were working hard to pay for these and even then our schoolbooks were not complete, not enough for us to have a full education.

'And black people were not people. We were not given our humanity.'

Older pupils listening to Radio Freedom from Mozambique and the banned World Service from the BBC brought in something else, not only news of international student unrest but direct evidence of the deformed nature of the terrible thing they were receiving in the name of education as blacks in South Africa.

The range of knowledge in people's conversations over the airwaves, both the amount of general information they had, and the confidence and fluency of their voices, revealed what people in South Africa were not getting:

'It was wrong to call what we received in our schools education.' Tebello says. 'Some people read English books, but in politics, in history, in social science, we had nothing.'

Hungry for more, for the confidence and knowledge of the voices coming from the radio, by May something had to give. Something had to be given:

'Only a spark was necessary to light the whole thing, to make it explode. And we were ready. By June, everything was moving forward.'

In Tebello's words on the 16th they 'grasped the fleeting moment. It was like electricity' he said. 'We jumped, shouted, we sang. It was wonderful. We had decided enough was enough and we were acting. We were speaking the truth. We were saying what was happening to us as young blacks in South Africa and what had happened to our parents was wrong. The powder keg had exploded.'

The acclaim for the March was overwhelming. Once the people who were at home that day saw the placards and thousands of young people, joyful for a change, leaping, clapping, singing together, they gave their approval. He recalls old ladies coming out of their houses as the students passed by and ululating their support, saying to the throng of marching young people: 'We are old, but you see, the time has come.'

'Boys *and* girls marched. It was a girl who nominated me to be one of the leaders of the organising committee for the march. Us leaders, we had some protection, two or three people who would watch us. And a girl, Anna Ganzin, was one of the people who protected me. She is late [dead] now.'

He recalls hearing that the police had fired shots, and appealing for the marchers to stay calm and also to stay put:

'We were not going to run away.'

Did they expect confrontation?

'Yes. But we didn't know their reaction would be so hostile.'

Tebello, like Murphy and many others who were part of the rapid, orderly planning of this March knew the police would arrive. But because the event was so well planned and built up with such unity and coherence by so many people, they thought they would carry the day, be allowed to march through Orlando West and say their piece. It is all they wanted. Their belief in their cause, their youth, their exhilaration to be doing something at last out of years of their own and their parents' exhaustion, meant they did not countenance what actually happened.

Tebello still expected there would be change in South Africa after this, that against all the odds it would occur. It would take fourteen years of people like him being in exile to bring it about. Like the thousands of others who took part in this and following protests, within a short time of the Uprising he had to leave the country.

The ANC in exile, its members dispersed overseas, notably to places like the UK, the States, Russia, Germany, had used well-worn routes to flee South Africa. Using its underground network within the country, individual contacts helped the class of '76 to flee. In clusters of half a dozen or so people, they were taken across borders through neighbouring countries like Lesotho, Botswana, Swaziland, Mozambique.

This then led either to army training or to education set up round the world, mainly through UN scholarships. Tebello did both over the next fourteen years. He was in the army and was also used as a spokesperson for the anti-apartheid movement world-wide. A good speaker, he told roomfuls of strangers what was happening in his country. Pictures of him, fetched by Jabu, show a tall, slender young man shaking hands with officials in Stockholm, London, New York.

He and Jabu seem happy together and he turns to her when he says that the journey, terrible as it was, was worth it. He would do it again, because it was right, because he spoke the truth in his terms and because, along the way, he found his wife.

Recalling their early life together in Swaziland and Mozambique, where he was last in exile before returning to South Africa in 1990, it was fraught though. As happened with Tsietsi Mashinini, Tebello had been branded a terrorist by the apartheid regime and, with spies all round, Jabu was warned she was going out with a dangerous man.

Easy-going, warm-hearted, Jabu smiles as she says: 'There were a lot of stories about him. People were telling me: "Whew, this guy has got lots of guns and he's wanted in South Africa."

'And when I was going out with him for a long time people were asking me: "Doesn't he sleep with guns?"

'"What guns?" I said to them. "I've never seen any guns."'

If you ask the people who were exiled about their feelings of being suddenly away from the only home they had known, there is a blank, like a silent compartment inside. They do not respond to questions about loneliness, isolation, difficulty of adapting in strange countries, some – like Sweden, Norway and Finland – with languages they did not speak.

They do not talk, in retrospect, of missing their families and of having no news from home. They seemed only to know they had to move on. The condition of the apartheid regime so oppressive, their families so vulnerable, they could not afford the finer feelings of need, yearning, loss.

Despite no direct contact with his family in these fourteen years in exile for fear of reprisals on them, Tebello's family did not escape apartheid's wrath. His elder brother, Jerry, taken into custody, Tebello says he was framed for a murder he did not commit. There was a stay of execution for five years because of the appeals and evidence presented, but eventually Jerry was hanged in 1982.

Tebello has kept some treasured documents, including poems he and others wrote of the time before he left South Africa. Like all banned material, they could have resulted in his arrest and imprisonment. As it is, he has saved them, almost thirty years on, preserved in a plastic bag.

The most striking is an A4-size bound publication from the NECC (National Education Crisis Committee). Set up by some of the elders in Soweto, the committee provided education after the burning, chaos and the closing of schools. A school workbook produced by this committee carries first-hand accounts of the day, plus written questions and exercises.

Called *What is History?*, partly torn, with pages missing, it includes a poem by R. Camhee, entitled 'Two Pairs of Eyes'.

Two pairs of eyes
met on a sultry morning

one belonged
to uniformed authority
equipped for a siege

the other
to a uniformed girl
fresh and neat

one pair flashed a dam
of instructions

the other was agleam
with defiance

one pair
pinned its hopes
on a baton

the other smiled
and said:
. . . you are afraid . . .

Tebello has a mantra, then and now, that 'speaking the truth changes a situation'. A religious man, his long-held conviction is that the development of a person or a nation happens if you begin from a true place. If you begin from a false place, a lie, your journey will not end well.

For him, the truth about the Uprising and what happened to the people who took part has not yet been spoken or publicly acknowledged. They wanted education and, through this, democracy in their country, the right to use their minds, and the truth is, he says, that democracy has not arrived in South Africa yet. Nor has free education.

Talking of the present ANC government Tebello says:

'Here, in South Africa, our people do not choose a representative. The MPs are appointed from above, so they are not independent and the community cannot challenge them.'

As for education:

'Children can't go to school if you do not have the money to send them. We are still waiting.'

This conversation will continue, but it is lunch-time. We have been in Soweto less than twelve hours, four of them spent asleep. The township's story from the past and its presence today through the people whose home we are sitting in, is alive, the issues as relevant as they were thirty years ago.

We will come back a number of times to discuss them, to see Jabu and Tebello and to talk. Their place will be our cup-of-tea-and-a-slice-of-cake stop on our way up and down the hill from Neo's near the bottom to the main road half a mile away at the top, and, if you turn right a few roads after Mandela's house, the Hector Pieterson Museum. We will walk it dozens of times.

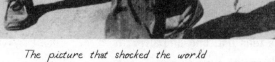

The picture that shocked the world

Sam Nzima

Chapter Thirteen

THE PICTURE

Soweto, Monday morning 20th September 2004

Approaching the Hector Pieterson Museum I am full of anticipation of the Museum itself, and the chance to see Freedom
again and to meet Andile and Isaac in a few hours' time.

The Museum houses the story of the Uprising in words
and in pictures on glass, slate, stone. The words, especially,
are measured. No need for high drama. The story speaks for
itself.

Photographs forbidden, I ask at the desk for permission to
jot down phrases, to take notes for a book and this is allowed.

The outline of what happened, which I first spotted here
a year back, is by now familiar to me from a digest of newspaper reports, documents, letters and books.

The aftermath is outlined too, police raiding classrooms
to capture the student leaders and taking action against the
black press which was keeping the story alive, banning eighteen publications by the end of 1977.

By this time most black organisations were banned and their
leaders detained. Also by this time, however, the writing on the
walls tells us, 'The Department of Bantu Education dropped
Afrikaans as a medium of instruction in African schools.'

Sitting in the Museum entrance on a rectangle of what feels, by its warmth, like soapstone, the remembered experience of church-height again, light falling in from tall windows and, just outside, behind the admissions desk, the small, bare sunlit courtyard and the scattered bricks.

On the clear glass window looking out onto this, words are written in red:

> We have entered the night to tell our tale,
> To listen to those who have not spoken.
> We who have seen our children die in the morning,
> Deserve to be listened to.
>
> Mazisi Kunene

And, as you come in, large letters, also on glass:

> An individual life can change a society.

I will learn later that the museum owes much of its design to the Holocaust Museum in Washington DC where a team of people from Soweto, including one of Neo's near neighbours, Shadrack Motau, went to research the development of this building. The written material is based on archival accounts which had escaped destruction, notably from Witz University.

Outside though, the story is told in a single photograph. At an angle, turned away so that you cannot immediately see it, either from the road, or the entrance, is a black and white picture, larger than life-size, which depicts what happened in Soweto that day.

Of the three figures in it, a tall youth is running. His handsome face open to the world, anguished and almost unbelieving, has come to symbolise the courage and the tremendous quality of Soweto's young people.

The girl by his side, younger, much shorter, is trying desperately to keep up with him as he runs literally for dear life, for the third figure in this picture, carried almost effortlessly in the tall boy's arms, is a slight, thin child, his limp body heavily bleeding.

Of the people here, the youngest, Hector, who was twelve, died a few moments after the picture was taken, the boy carrying him, Mbuyisa, fled for his life and has not been seen in Soweto since. Thirty years later he is presumed dead.

The third, a seventeen-year-old girl, Antoinette, you will find a few yards away. So little changed, you would recognise her if you stopped for a moment, as she works issuing entrance tickets and answering visitors' questions in the light-brick building which bears her dead brother's name.

Inside the Hector Pieterson Museum, she sees every day a slightly different version of the photograph outside. Taken a split second later, her head is thrown back as her hand reaches to touch her brother.

How these photographs survived is remarkable. News photographers forbidden to take pictures of the police in action, the man who took them had his camera opened by the police and his film exposed minutes later.

But Sam Nzima, a staff journalist for the *World* newspaper in nearby Jo'burg, had been around a while. As soon as he had taken the frames of Mbuyisa, quickly he wound off the film, got it out of the camera and was loading another blank from his pocket almost at the same time. Bent over and bending over further to scratch his ankle, the used film was tucked into the side of his sock.

When the police got to him and forced him to open up, the newly wound-on film was exposed. Shortly after, the one from his sock was discreetly passed to the office driver and driven straight to Jo'burg.

Sam had been dropped off that Wednesday morning before six, the editor having got wind of something happening. Thousands of pupils already gathered, it was an amazing sight, nearly all in school uniforms, grey, black, some with white shirts, many with woolly hats, arriving minute by minute, feeding from side roads into the main body of people. Keeping one of the 'Afrikaans must be abolished' placards in his eyeline, Sam marched with them from his drop-off point at Naledi High.

The police had been arriving alongside the marchers, but their presence at the head of the March was felt strongly, some say at nine am, others at ten. The accounts from marchers and journalists alike say the same thing about the atmosphere at this stage, it was a happy one. Children report being unafraid of the police on this day because they were all together and were not doing anything wrong.

Other reports confirm this, that the schoolchildren were

singing and dancing, that they were peaceful and that they were given no warning of what was to follow when a police chief threw, or let something loose, into the crowd. Most say this was a tear-gas canister, others that the first thing sent into the crowd was a snarling dog. Within minutes, shots were fired – and the first children fell.

What Sam saw was a police commander arrive with a convoy of cars, take out a gun and, unprovoked, shoot straight into the crowd.

It was then bedlam. Hector had fallen, as had other children. Police dogs released, either then or before to frighten them further, in fear and fury a group of young people, girls and boys, tackled one of these, an alsatian called Shaka. Trained to strike fear in people by jumping for the throat, this one was trailing its lead and, picking up its chain, children throttled and stoned it to death.

But Sam had seen something else. Trying to get near the fallen children, people running, screaming, he saw a youth, not in school uniform, heading fast *into* this scene, towards a child's body on the ground. Almost without breaking stride, scooping the child up, he then kept going.

Eighteen-year-old Mbuyisa Makhubu was not on the March that day, which is why, instead of his Orlando High blazer and school uniform, he is wearing dungarees. At home with his mother Elizabeth, and sister, hearing what sounded like gunshots, and knowing it was the day of the protest, he sprinted out of the house, through shrubland, along a path to where the shots were coming from.

In the few months he remained in Soweto after this, Mbuyisa never spoke to his family of what he saw or felt. What Sam saw through his viewfinder was his boyish figure make swift progress through the side of the police lines and pick up a child's inert body. Continuing to move at speed with the child in his arms, he ran towards Sam in full view and was joined by another figure.

Antoinette, standing at the top of her street when she heard the shots, stood still in shock. The next thing she recalls is seeing a boy she had never met before, and would not meet again, running hard towards her carrying what she saw was a child's body in his arms.

As he came nearer she recognised by his shoes that the child being carried was her brother. Not knowing what Mbuyisa did, that there was a nearby health clinic he was heading towards, she ran alongside breathlessly telling him who Hector was. In one of the half a dozen frames of this tableau of three people, taken split seconds apart, she is trying to make contact, touching her brother's leg as she runs along at full tilt.

In the moments it took all this to happen, another person had seen Hector lifted from the ground. Also a journalist, she had a car and a driver with her, and, as Mbuyisa and Antoinette headed towards her, she urged them quickly, get the child in the back seat of the car for him to be taken to hospital.

Of the now-famous frames Sam took of those few

moments, the last shows Hector being lowered into the seat and, as Sam describes it, 'the breath had gone from him. You could see it. As they laid him down, his life had gone.'

The photograph taken of Mbuyisa's action that day did more to turn hearts and minds against the apartheid regime than millions of previously written – and banned – words and the police raided home after home to try and find this boy. The fact that he was not in school uniform and therefore hardly likely to be a leader, escaped them.

Mbuyisa had to move on. Steering clear of his own house for fear of reprisals on his family, he never slept in his home or stayed with his family again. Although not a student leader and not part of the protest, he was one of the most wanted. People who saw him from time to time say he had lost weight, looked very changed and was eventually seen no more.

A year later, a letter to his mother Elizabeth via a family friend said he was in Nigeria and having difficulty settling into this new strange land. Another received in June 1978 said he was ill. And then nothing. The family was eventually told he was dead, but were given no details of where he was buried and there were conflicting details of how he died.

The continuing tragedy of the story of this picture, seen by hundreds of millions of people, is the price paid for it. The child, Hector, was dead within minutes of being picked up off the ground. The eighteen-year-old boy, Mbuyisa, who tried to rescue him, was not on the March that day because he told a friend he thought there would be trouble. He is presumed dead. Antoinette, herself a mother, is silent now, saying only there is nothing more to be said about those times.

And Sam. Sam had to flee in fear of his life. Losing his home and his job, he has not lived in Soweto since. For a while he worked taking wedding pictures hundreds of miles north of here, but it was not what he was used to doing. Then, he ran a bottle store. Now, in his seventies, and a grandfather, he lives with his wife not far from Kruger Park.

Speaking on the phone, he says he does not like talking about that time. The next day the police came to his office to arrest him and to try and get Mbuyisa's address. His editor saved his skin, intervening on his behalf, but then:

'Someone who was friendly to me in the police told me they were going to shoot me and say it was an accident. So I left Soweto because my life was in danger.

'The next year, the *World* newspaper was banned and they took all the pictures, all the photographs, and destroyed them.'

But this particular picture, or at least copies of it, had already flown. The South African Council of Churches printed 800 copies that Christmas and sent them overseas as Christmas cards. Their offices were raided too. It was shown in German churches, in British churches, and it became an iconic photograph, the one single image most associated with what happened to schoolchildren in Soweto that day.

It has brought Sam no feeling of accomplishment. Despite

its world-wide influence on people's minds and hearts, he says the human price paid for it was too high.

Nor, he says, did it initially bring him acclaim. He was employed by the Argus group as a photo-journalist at the time, so the photograph was not his. The newspaper was eventually sold in the late nineties to the Independent Group in London. Sam has since been given the copyright and people who want to re-use the image should, by law, gain his permission and pay him a fee to do so. He says:

'I didn't know the importance of the photograph I took. I was working in a battlefield. I quickly wound off the film and put it in my shoesock.'

Then life, events, history, took over. By that afternoon of June 16th the picture was on the front page of his local newspaper and, by the following day, half-way round the world.

Here, in Soweto, outside the Museum, on one of the many low ledges and sitting places, there are white words painted on mottled grey-pink and blue stone from Mbuyisa's mother, Elizabeth, who died earlier this year:

'Mbuyisa is or was my son. But he is not a hero. In my culture, picking up Hector is not an act of heroism. It was his job as a brother. If he left him on the ground and somebody saw him jumping over Hector, he would never be able to live here.'

Chapter Fourteen

A Meal at Motsoaledi

Motsoaledi Informal Settlement

Soweto, Monday afternoon 20th September 2004

Jabu picking up Manoli and me at Neo's on Monday afternoon to drive us to Freedom and his family, the Takashanas are two or three miles away from Neo and a world apart. There are street lights in Orlando West and, with its detached houses and tended gardens, parts of Vilakazi Street look as comfortable as a London suburb.

But where Freedom lives looks ancient in its starkness, recalling a time before cities were built, before electricity and modern ideas of comfort.

The small shacks off the wide dirt track are clustered in yards of between half a dozen and a dozen dwellings, some leaning against each other, some straight, others at an angle. One has a cream wall with a few dark blue and ochre diamonds painted carefully on the side as decoration. I notice the toilets again, which look like yellow phone boxes, positioned at the side of the track, about one every 100 yards.

Drawing up in the dust at the edge of this, the Motsoaledi Informal Settlement off the Old Potch Road, a guide arranged by Jabu comes to meet us, Siphiwe. The boys will be somewhere around, playing, Jabu tells us, and, meanwhile it is after four, he will go and fetch their father Isaac from where he works as a petrol attendant and bring him back to see us.

Walking down the dirt road we pass the water tap, people nearest to it with less carrying to do, even growing vegetables and flowers but, as we find out, the Takashanas live furthest away.

The dwelling where Freedom, Andile and Isaac live has no window. Made of the corrugated metal sheeting which is standard in squatter camps, it is a dark place. Burnt once, they do not know how, most of it is curled out of shape. Lips of thin metal turn up at the edges like old sticking plaster, and the wooden door, which has no hinge, is propped back against a bed. The roof, too is bent out of shape and in the dark interior chinks of light come through. Okay in the summer, but what about the cold winters and frequent rain?

In this one room, about nine feet by eight, the three of them sleep, eat, bathe, wash up, study, paint – as we see from slender paint brushes standing up in a bottle – and generally live their lives.

Manoli and I are carrying between us simple, practical gifts. A long strip of plastic cups for Isaac, dozens of pens for children we might meet, writing paper and exercise books. There are two special pens for Freedom and Andile, and two writing books, one in blue, the other in purple, hard-backed with silver glitters.

The books are a result of talking to Freedom a year ago when he had said how much he liked writing stories. We have brightly coloured socks from the plane as well, given out to wear instead of shoes on the long journey. 'Take everything you can,' a woman sitting next to us had said as we went to stick them in the seatback. 'In Soweto they can use everything.' So socks, packets of biscuits, nuts, chocolates, more plastic cups and, as an afterthought, some plastic bottles of water too.

In my luggage there are two reading books as well, one each for Freedom and Andile, written and signed by South African author Beverley Naidoo. Manoli is carrying two disposable cameras. She says she would be interested to see what kind of photographs the boys take. Also, she thinks they will enjoy using them.

We are standing outside the family's burnt house, deserted at the moment, but word travels fast round here, especially of the presence of two white women, and round the corner, on his own, comes the slight figure of Freedom.

I move to take a step forward in greeting, and stop. He is gazing doubtfully at me and I, too, hesitate. Which is how we stay for a moment, Freedom head on one side looking up at me quizzically. He is thin still, looks uncomfortable and does not seem to recognise me.

'Do you remember meeting me last year?'

He shakes his head.

'Have you had food today?'

'Yes,' he says in the clear serious voice I recall well.

'Are you still hungry?'

'Yes,' looking straight at me now, his expression deep, sad, 'I am hungry still.'

Moved by Freedom, as I was a year ago, by his gravity and the sense that he is old beyond his years, I notice how he is still held back. I had hoped the security of a regular meal may have brought about a change in this restraint. Perhaps it is too soon.

By this time we have the company of other children, Freedom's brother Andile among them. Almost two years older, he seems strong, calm and more confident than his brother. Around a dozen of us in all, children looking at us, chatting, playing, Freedom remains quiet.

And it occurs to me why he does not remember our meeting last year. As Tebello and others have described it, hunger produces light-headedness and an inability to take things in.

Is there anywhere we can find food for these children? I ask Siphiwe in a near repeat of my question a year ago. Yes, he says. Patricia, she has a big family and there is a shop to buy mealie and tripe. She will cook for the children. Asking him to let her know I will give her money of course, quickly counting heads, there are ten children at the moment. Fifteen plates then, in case more arrive.

Probably in her fifties or sixties, Patricia comes out of a home nearby and gives Manoli and me hugs before noisily setting to work. From somewhere inside a cluster of small homes, there are loud orders and clatters of plates.

As we chat to Siphiwe, to some men sitting nearby and to the children, Freedom is still withdrawn, listless almost, until a small girl tugs at his sleeve and, holding up her arms, asks to be picked up.

It is a lovely moment: Freedom, looking nine years old still, slender in faded yellow long-sleeved jumper and dark cut-off trousers, swinging a giggling two or three-year-old through the air, her laughter making him smile.

At last the food arrives, the mealie and tripe in large white china soup bowls, Patricia ordering the children to be careful not to break them, or there will be trouble. Telling them to wash their hands first, a small tin bath of water is fetched. They swish their hands in it, toddlers of two or three dipping in, then wiping damp fingers dry on their jumpers, fifteen-year-olds doing the same. Sitting on the step or on the ground, everyone eats carefully with their fingers.

As this is taking place, walking slowly round the side of the small compound where we are all gathered, Isaac arrives. A well-built man, in his late-fifties, around five foot nine, with a strong and kindly face, he has short grey hair and a matching trimmed moustache.

I watch as slowly he turns the corner of the wire fence enclosure and stands a few yards off, facing us now, taking in the scene. Wearing a long-sleeved blue plaid shirt and dark blue trousers he has a peaked cloth hat which, taking it off, he holds in his hand.

This is how he stays, gazing. It is how I stay too, enough restraint in me to keep from rushing forward. So we stand this way for a minute, until eventually I walk forward and slowly extend my hand.

I am glad to meet you I say.

And I am glad to meet you.

We stay still for what seems like quite a while. African handshakes being as they are, not shakes, but holds, one of my hands is in one of his, my other hand has arrived, unawares, on top, and his other on top in turn. So we stand like this, four hands and a squashed hat, Isaac calm, seeming as if he is in a pleasant dream. Then I wake up:

'You've been working. We have food here. Would you like some?'

'Thank you.' Isaac nods.

He is brought a bowl of food and the gathering continues, talk, laughter, Patricia coming out to hug Manoli and me again, almost lifting Manoli off her feet.

Meanwhile Freedom, having eaten, is beginning to take pictures with the gift Manoli has given him, the quality of waiting in him different with a camera in his hand. Looking quietly around he seems to compose what he wants, to pick his shot before pressing the shutter. In a photo that Manoli takes of him doing this, he is like someone who has held a camera for years, arms up, hands away from the lens, head slightly forward, knees a little bent, a natural bare-foot photographer.

Observing as best I can, standing back enjoying the scene, the homeliness, the warmth, the energy of it, there is much to take in, especially colour. Evening time, sunlight beginning to dip, an array of rich dark colours to fill the eye: ochre, sable, charcoal, ebony, copper, bronze. The light retreating fast now, as if running away, it takes out the depth of colour, leaving unlit shadows of grey and brown.

Darkness almost upon us, I have a short talk with Isaac before we leave. On my behalf, Jabu, who visits the family from time to time, has told Isaac of the book I am writing and has asked his permission for me to interview them all. I have been told this is fine, but I would like to make sure there are no misunderstandings.

Asking Isaac if he knows I am writing a book about the Uprising in Soweto thirty years ago and their own lives in the township now, he nods. Is it all right, I ask, that I interview him and the boys?

That is fine, he confirms.

And do I have his permission to take Freedom and Andile to Neo's house where she will interpret for us while we do an interview?

Yes, Isaac says. He is happy for that to happen.

What I notice about Isaac is the stillness in him. You have the impression of a dignified and sincere man. Darkness arrived, Manoli and I preparing to leave, he looks at me squarely:

'Thank you for the help you are giving me and my family.'

I am not sure how to respond and, after a moment, say I am glad to give it.

'You are a good person,' he says, seriously, before we turn away.

Chapter Fifteen

THE OTHER PICTURE AND MORE SILENCE

On guard

The burning of evidence in the seventies, the banning of newspapers, raiding of offices, went on apace. But without knowing it, the apartheid regime had already destroyed a photograph which could have changed the course of history.

Shortly after Hector was shot, a handful of schoolchildren in another part of the crowd retaliated. Sam Nzima does not remember whether or not they were in school uniform. They may have been tsotsis who had infiltrated the marchers, but even so, whether in uniform or not, some children carried knives.

What Sam saw, and snapped another half a dozen frames

of, was a group of young people leaping on a policeman and slitting his throat. Part of a contingent of police reinforcements who arrived in an open van, this policeman was the last to step out and was brought to the ground and killed almost instantly.

Sam said:

'When the police reinforcements arrived in these open vans, they did not expect the youth to retaliate so strongly.

'What I saw was children slaughtering a policeman, cutting his throat like a goat as he came out of the van.'

Then, as Sam moved off, police made him open his camera for the second time that day and expose the just-taken shots.

The value to the apartheid regime of having in its possession a photograph showing black schoolchildren killing a policeman by slitting his throat was incalculable. In the regime's hands it could have gone a long way to turning back the tide of international anti-apartheid feeling which followed.

This picture destroyed, the emblematic image of June 16th remains Mbuyisa's youthful, open-faced figure running with Hector in his arms. So inherently did this capture the spirit of the day that the other photographs which were also true, of the stone-throwing petrol-bombing rampage which is what the protest developed into by nightfall, became transitory asides to the enduring nature of this one image.

What is known of Mbuyisa's fate after he fled Soweto is tracked in a video, *What happened to MBUYISA?* directed by Feizel Mamdoo.

He fled from South Africa and, taking one of the handful

of well-worn routes out of the country, stayed in Botswana for a while with a teacher and his family. This is where, eventually, he fathered a child. But, before his son was born he was given one of the UN scholarships available to young people fleeing areas of strife.

Providing a framework of basic education and skills for displaced young people, Mbuyisa was sent on a scholarship operating in Nigeria, which is where the letter to his mother, Elizabeth was sent from. Received in June 1978 and saying he was ill, it was the last known contact.

The silences, of all kinds, which followed '76 and those who supported it all over the country were deep, long and still exist. The trauma experienced by a community in Soweto and by a black and coloured community countrywide, was too much to speak of and remains, in the lives of many people, voiceless: an inner constraint.

A white man, an anti-apartheid campaigner living near the Cape at the time, recalls:

'It was like constant pressure on the brain. The silence went on and on, to protect your families mainly. What was happening in South Africa at that time was a horrible secret and we were all implicated in the destruction of people, in the genocide, the starvation.

'After Soweto kicked off in the mid-late seventies, I saw trucks with bodies in going to the dumping yards. I was a student at the time. I didn't tell my mother, or my sister. I didn't tell anyone else about this.

'Wherever you were in public if there more than a couple of you, you knew someone would be informing. We kept our mouths shut. It was dreadful.'

People who fled have been called a silenced generation who 'talk in whispers to each other to this day'. For most there was no contact at all for fourteen years with the mothers, fathers, siblings they had left behind, nor with each other. Those who did not join the army in Angola were individually scattered round the world with no thought to ties of friendship. They did not return until 1990, following Nelson Mandela's release and the beginning of the end of apartheid.

The student exiles' double tragedy, as well as the sudden loss of home and familiarity, was their ill-preparedness for life in a world outside South Africa. Candlelight readings of Dickens and Shakespeare, TEACH and LEARN aside, most of the youth of South Africa had little more than the thin gruel of Bantu Education to sustain them.

Although the shining lights of the class of '76 had bright minds and courageous hearts, they were ill-fitted for fourteen years in exile. There were exceptions, but people who met young exiles on their travels in the UK and in Europe were aware how un-streetwise they were and how difficult it was for them to integrate their extraordinary experiences into their new lives.

In the townships they had fled, however, in Jo'burg, in the Cape, in the years which followed 1976, things got much worse as the ideals of the people who had left were obliterated by mindless violence. Mob rule by the young.

There was a saying in South Africa that there was no middle of the road, no middle ground any more for discussion, no place for democratic debate and freedom of thought. It is what a schoolchild may have had in mind in an anonymous poem written in 1976, called 'The Aftermath':

> The students have marched
> Some have died
> There was smoke everywhere
>
> The smoke has cleared
> The buildings have burned
> There are ruins everywhere
>
> Our absent leaders know it
> Our present 'leaders' don't –
> That the aftermath is brewing.

Many schools closed, teachers who were sympathetic to students also flown and the silent majority voiceless with grief, a minority of vociferous people speaking a false, whipped-up message stepped into the vacuum and a long, bloody aftermath followed. Bedlam followed cruelty followed torture followed mayhem.

One of the many false claims made as a result of June 16th was the destruction of a revered tradition, the respect shown by young people to their elders. Indeed, sorrowing the deaths of hundreds of children in Soweto, some parents accused themselves of cowardice, of making the youth do their job for them and to die young as a result.

There was despair among parents, an abject grief on grief as they mourned the loss of young life and the draining away of their own vitality by decades of abuse. In the NECC publication saved by Tebello there is a poem from such a person, Mafika Gwala, called 'Old Man Nxele's Remorse, 20 June 1976':

> Sons,
> They are gunning down
> our children
> in Soweto;
> What more
> are we still living for?

The need was for time and peace to find what to say, what to do, what to think next. Which is what was not available. Swiftly, into this temporary hiatus, at a time when the youth leaders had fled and the older generation was in grief, stepped some wild and heavily damaged young opportunists.

Truth did a triple somersault in South Africa by the eighties. Battered, tormented, curled up, its ragged body was heaved into the air. As well as white on black crime, black on black crime, a new category of major crime appeared, committed by rampaging youths and children on each other and especially their elders.

South African psychologist Brian Rock, now working in

London, writes about childhood trauma in South Africa in a book called *Spirals of Suffering*. Working alongside a Commission headed by South African Judge Richard Goldstone, veteran of the International War Crimes Tribunal, Rock looked at children's plight.

In particular, his work investigated the devastating effects of decades of violence on the behaviour of children, some of whom themselves became violent. Writing of a thirteen-year-old boy 'General' in Soweto running an army of 1,400 'soldiers', Rock states:

'While their activities were targeted against the State, they also turned in on their own townships . . . against anyone who met with their disapproval . . .

'They engaged in night patrols, embarked upon intimidation and extortion campaigns, and issued death threats, which in many instances left the residents of certain communities isolated and helpless.'

Describing how in the 1980s 'leadership by "the youth"' involved the staging of civic courts in which punishments were meted out, a typical illustration of the workings of these courts, headed by self-appointed twelve and thirteen-year-olds, was as follows:

'. . . men between the ages of 34 and 63 were hauled in front of a "people's court" at three o'clock in the morning in Soweto . . . They were sentenced to 500 lashes each, stripped naked in front of ten-year-olds, spreadeagled over a drum, and flogged.'

The youth who fled the country with their ideals for education left behind activities like these, and, in Soweto itself, Winnie Mandela ran her notorious Football Club, supposedly set up for her own protection but in fact responsible for the torture and the murder of at least one child in her back yard.

On the streets, as well as the tsotsis, there were the 'hoodies', named not after clothing, but because they were the so-called Robin Hoods, robbing the white rich to give to the black poor. But as life in the townships deteriorated into a blood-letting nightmare which the apartheid regime was happy to turn a blind eye to, in time the hoodies robbed everyone, *especially* the black poor.

The impetus that had driven the class of '76 to protest in order to save and to use their minds was absent in the mob rule which followed and the townships descended into infernos of violence where it was a miracle for good people to survive.

Rian Malan, a white journalist working in Jo'burg as a crime reporter, hating apartheid, yet, as the going got rough, afraid for the colour of his white skin, describes it in his book *My Traitor's Heart*:

'There was so much horror in my country, and it came in so many forms. There was the white horror, the horror of black protesters shot down in the streets. But there was another kind of horror too, the horror blacks inflicted on one another . . .

'Yes, things are bad now. Yes, they can get worse . . .' And they did.

Some of South Africa's worst cruelty was meted out by gangs of children, many of whom claimed to have so-called political causes. When Rian Malan tried to get to the bottom of the rivalry between two Soweto gangs, members as young as fourteen who burned people alive, what he was told was that one gang had taken Steve Biko (murdered in police custody in 1977) as their 'father' and the other gang had taken their 'leader' as Nelson Mandela.

Violently opposed to each other's ideologies – their ways of dealing with apartheid – they killed each other and each other's friends and families in the process.

The biggest single influence on the uprising in June 1976 was the life, work and illegally passed-on words of Steve Biko and his idea of 'conscientisation' – expressing conscience through education and self-development. One of *his* main influences was the Brazilian educator Paulo Freire, whose work involved educating the complete person and producing 'a means by which man discovers himself and his potential'. When invited to contribute to a book on black theology (*Black Theology: The South African Voice*) Biko echoes this in writing:

'. . . the black man wishes to explore his surroundings and test his possibilities – in other words to make his freedom real . . . At the heart of this kind of thinking is the realisation by blacks that the most potent weapon in the hands of the oppressor is the mind of the oppressed. If one is free at heart, no man-made chains can bind one to servitude . . .'

Defending his stated position that blacks had to do this their own way, without white interference, he writes:

'Some will charge that we are racist . . . Blacks have had enough experience as objects of racism not to wish to turn the tables . . .

'In time we shall be in a position to bestow upon South Africa the greatest gift possible – a more human face.'

Tragic enough that two of South Africa's giant figures in the battle against apartheid should have their names invoked in the killing of blacks. But with Biko dead by this time, and Mandela serving a life sentence in prison, the leaders of '76 scattered around the world, hoodies on the street, the only thing left for ordinary peace-loving blacks in South Africa in the grim years of the eighties was silence.

Those who knew the middle of the road, who could see what was happening on both sides, that the black minority had become as vicious as the white, were silent for fear of being labelled sell-outs and hauled before the mindless courts of cruel, uneducated children.

Out of all of it, the burnings of people and property, betrayal, perversion, shootings, tanks, looting, and all the bedlam of war let loose on a township of little more than a million people, out of the ash, fire, atrocity and grief, tens of thousands, young and old, kept their counsel and waited silently for this, too, to pass.

Chapter Sixteen

TEA AND PHOTOGRAPHS AT NEO'S

Neo

Soweto, Tuesday 21st September 2004

Neo has an air of containment about her. She carries her life within her face, which is expressive and can also express distance. She goes a long way off sometimes, not on the outside, to send you away, but on the inside.

She is deep and you can see, if you care to observe, the miles she has travelled in more than two decades as a widow. I have seen her before, walking down the roads of my childhood, her quality of waiting, of being there, someone taking care of the moments, carrying the memories, while you are gone.

And today she wants us gone. Out of the way. Without us knowing, what she will do when we leave is make her well-cared-for home even more inviting for her young visitors, Freedom and Andile, who are coming to tea.

She will make sure the over-size TV in the small living room she sets aside for guests is plugged in properly and working at the touch of a button. She will clean away my bits of stuff, spare film, tape jackets and ubiquitous pens, from the low glass table and re-arrange the antimacassars on the high-backed chairs beautifully covered in a patterned fabric of grey-blues and olive-greens.

She will experiment with opening and closing the heavy curtains a little and will leave them inbetween. She will close the door of the bedroom Manoli and I share just off this lounge, after taking a peek inside to see what I have done with the bolster. My having hidden it in the wardrobe as usual, she will put it back on the bed.

Bedroom door closed, guest lounge settled, kitchen tidy, she will then change into a button-through black linen dress with a plain red cardigan, glossy lipstick to match and shiny black high-heeled shoes.

We have been here a few days and it seems like a lifetime, so much are we at home. Quickly we have established a routine of breakfast at eight, out of the house by nine, return by nightfall if we make it, which we sometimes do not.

In the evening, a meal in or out with Neo, a chat with local people in houses nearby, perhaps a visit to Neo's local drinking and dancing spot, her favourite shebeen and one of us, usually me, calling it a day by falling asleep sitting up. So full is our stay of interviews, phonecalls, people talking to us on the street, impressions, observations, trying to take things in, that most times we are gone to the world before midnight.

Here and now we are off to Motsoaledi Settlement again, to bring the boys back for Neo to translate for us. While their English is adequate, Neo speaks their languages, Xhosa and Sotho.

When Isaac named his two children, the first was called Andile, which means flourishing and 'the family is growing'. The name of the second child, Nkululeko, means freedom because 'you want people to be free' Isaac tells me. In choosing their names he wanted to create something meaningful for his children which is true as well to who they are:

'You musn't give a wrong name.'

A child who was called flourishing, which is how Andile was as a baby and properly named therefore, would grow, develop and provide substance. The next child, the smaller one, who moved around more, would make them free. With the joint attributes in their names, growth and freedom, the boys would bring good things to each other and would have between them a good possibility in life.

They are obviously close, though very different. Andile is confident and has grown in the year since Sue sent the first picture of him and Freedom together. As well as seeming calm, he is physically strong.

Freedom is less robust. Noticeably 'an old soul', more reflective, he watches and is, ironically with the name he has, held back as I was before Iringa helped me to come out of myself. He is not unconfident. Freedom seems to know who he is, but does not willingly push himself forward or take the lead.

Except . . .

We are told it is a big treat for children in Soweto to be given sweets. Leaving aside our Western concerns about tooth rot and bad eating habits, we take to carrying them in our pockets. We hand one of the two big packets of chocolates and sweets we have brought on our second visit to Motsoaledi over to Siphiwe to give to Isaac for later and the other ends up with Freedom to be shared out and eaten now. Here he is, bag in hand, facing a queue of a dozen children waiting their turn, Freedom in charge counting out the goodies, two each.

Siphiwe, who lives in the next yard, had told us on the way to the house that the Takashanas are good people, the boys are good boys, and the family does not deserve its bad luck.

What does he mean by the boys being good?

They are polite and they don't get into fights.

And the bad luck? Does he mean the house being burned or something else?

Isaac will tell us what we can see, that the boys have no mother. And that is very sad for them.

Asked how he knows about this sadness and if the boys

speak about it, Siphiwe shakes his head. But all children need a mother because a mother does special things for a child, he tells Manoli and me. Other children here and in school have mothers and they speak about their mother doing this and that for them:

'And these boys don't have a mother. I know it makes them sad.'

Talking to Isaac later, the burnt house is not the only piece of bad luck in his life, although you would not know it from his face which, in repose, bears no sign of rancour.

The family arrived in Soweto in 1992 with Freedom just a few months old, having left the Eastern Cape where Isaac and his parents were cattle farmers. Nearly all the cattle in the vast farming region of the Transkei had died in a few years from a disease called locally umbendeni, similar to red water or gall sickness. The region never recovered from this and Isaac, seeing no prospect of providing for his wife and two small boys, brought them to Soweto where there was a chance of work.

The Takashana family already knew Soweto because of the Uprising. In the seventies Isaac's elder sister lived in the township, fleeing back to Transkei in 1976 because her oldest child was involved in the protest that day. Although not hurt, in an attempt to strike fear in people and round up the ringleaders, the police hounded the family as they did hundreds of others. Fearing for their lives, mother and son left Soweto and caught a bus south.

Arriving back in Mvuzi Location near the small farming

town of Mount Frere, the whole family had a conference at which it was decided mother and son should stay put. Afraid that the two may have been followed by the security police, they would all need to be on the alert for signs of trouble. It was a year or more before the anxiety went away and the family moved about without looking over their shoulders and taking the precaution of not straying far from the house on their own.

But in Soweto, fifteen years later, Isaac's wife, much younger than him and with new people to distract her, leaves him, initially taking the boys with her. In a short while, he learns from neighbours she is not looking after them well. Although they are still little older than babies in African terms, they are left alone with no one to care for them and Isaac decides to take the highly unusual step of claiming them.

Kidnapping them is what he calls it and having accomplished it at a time when Freedom is only three and Andile almost five, his wife, their mother, moves away and has not been seen or heard from again. The indignation Isaac feels about this still evident, I ask no further. Since that time, with no female relatives on hand to help with caring for the boys, Isaac has done the domestic work of cooking and cleaning and has held down a job.

He works at a petrol station earning R400 a month, less than £9 a week for working nine to ten hours a day and a half day on Saturday, with only Sundays off. This is poor, even by South African standards and, according to Union officials, is a third of what he should be paid. But his bosses are not interested in paying more. He can take the job or leave it. With unemployment running at 50 per cent in the township, he stays on.

Under these conditions, it is a full schedule: up soon after five to get the boys washed, dressed and with breakfast in their stomachs before their mile-long walk to school, then himself to work, walking around half a mile by eight, finishing usually around 5.30 pm. Yes, it is a lot to do, he tells me, but it is worth it to have the boys with him. His neighbours are kind and with my help the family has enough to eat.

It is getting late, the warmth of the day fading. We were due at Neo's at four and it is gone half past five. Jabu driving us and the boys back to Orlando West, coming in towards Neo's by a different route, from the top of the street down, Freedom spots the sign to Mandela's house mid-way along the Vilakazi.

'I have never been to Mandela's house,' he announces in his usual serious voice.

I think of going back, but believe it will be closed and we are late for Neo. It is not fair to keep her waiting any longer. On the street outside her house, looking around, almost dark now, Freedom thinks everything is beautiful. 'The place is beautiful' is what he says, standing in the garden. Walking up the road later, he will look around him at a tree, a garden, a house and say: 'It is beautiful.'

For now, though, he and Andile are eating cake and drinking squash in Neo's kitchen, having first helped her to lay the table. As she translates my questions into a mixture of Xhosa and Sotho, to my surprise, Freedom's dream is to win the lottery so that when he grows older he will have his own business. Also surprisingly for his slight build, he wants to be a rugby player.

Andile, on the other hand, wants to be a fireman because 'the house had a fire'. They came home and their things were gone. He wishes, too, to be like Mandela, whom he looks up to. They both enjoy stories and Andile likes painting. They do not like fighting and when this happens, as it does in the settlement, they walk away.

Freedom meanwhile, is waiting to take a picture of Neo, and takes many minutes, reaching surreptitiously for the camera, then taking his hand away, then eventually, having lined it up in his mind, suddenly picking it up and taking the best picture we have of her. Neo looks thirty-five in this photograph, what with the way Freedom has caught her beautifully smiling and with her being all dressed up.

Enough of sitting down, I offer them a choice: they can either watch TV for half an hour or we can walk up to Mandela's house. It will be closed, so they will only see it from the outside through the security bars.

There is no contest. We are on the street, walking up towards the place where Mandela used to live before Neo can switch off the well-primed telly.

'This is the first time for me to see Mandela's house,' pronounces Freedom gravely to us all, and to the pavement ahead, which is where he is looking in studious manner, as we get nearer.

He wants to know if Mandela will be inside and is disappointed to learn he lives elsewhere.

'I would like to meet him,' he says.

'What would you do if you did meet him?' I ask.

'I would shake his hand.'

'Would you say anything to him?'

He shakes his head.

'And Andile? What would you do if you met Mandela?'

'I would shake his hand.'

'Why?'

'Without him we wouldn't be where we are today.'

Outside the small gated house with its large tree in the garden obscuring most of the front, and in the dark, Freedom takes more pictures. Returning to Neo's, she produces wrapped-up cake for later and I give the boys a hug. Saying goodbye the day before, aware of their age and the fact that I had appeared from afar and would disappear again by next week, I had asked Freedom and Andile if they would like a handshake or a hug.

'Both,' they had said straight off.

Chapter Seventeen

TRUTH TELLERS AND LETTER WRITERS

Carol and Andile

On his visit before my trip to Soweto, Paul Trewhela had left me his letter to Archbishop Tutu of June 1990 asking for evidence of ANC abuse in Angola to be brought into the open. Detailing his knowledge of killings by the ANC security forces and of Quatro, the infamous ANC prison in Angola, he had appealed to the Archbishop to intervene.

Co-editing *Searchlight South Africa* providing Paul Trewhela with a unique view of what followed on from the rebellion on June 16th, he told me:

'Once '76 had happened there was a strong need to get young people out of the country and then to enlist them. An effective way of doing this was to get them into military units. In this way the '76 generation was chewed up by the Cold War in Africa.'

Information about the ANC in Angola not coming reliably into the public domain until 1990, evidence of what happened in the time inbetween, and in the crucial years between 1976 and 1988, initially came from the letters sent by the class of '76.

Young people fleeing the apartheid regime sent for military training, mostly in East Germany, they returned to the ANC Command's headquarters in Lusaka, Zambia, as MK soldiers (the military wing of the ANC). Despatched to camps in Angola, these new recruits were confronted by the dreadful conditions their letters eventually brought to light: that they were beaten, imprisoned and tortured for asking for improved conditions, including medical care; that people were tortured and killed for questioning the excesses and illegal behaviour of those in command; that they were given dreadful food while their 'superiors' ate well; that senior ANC officers were involved in diamond and drug smuggling and the raping of women soldiers. Recruits who spoke out against this were beaten, sometimes to death.

The handful of people named in print for these abuses are always the same. They include army commander, Joe Modise; Chief of the ANC Security Services, Mzwandile Piliso; and National Political Commissar of the ANC, Andrew Masondo. Oliver Tambo, the President in exile, is heavily criticised for not intervening.

Malnutrition and deaths from beatings leading to increas-
ing desertions, when a formal request in 1980 for an ANC
conference (there had not been one for eleven years) was
denied, the MK lost hope. By 1984, they refused to take
orders any more.

Those who were there say that by this time mutiny had
spread to around 90 per cent of the MK guerrillas in Angola.
Eight years in exile in appalling conditions, doing nothing
useful to fight apartheid, being starved and beaten while the
organisation they were fighting for became more corrupt and
brutal, was too much to take.

People thought to be the ringleaders of the mutiny were
sent to the organisation's prison, Quatro, in northern Angola.
It is there they were tortured and where a number died.

Survivors were kept in Quatro until 1988 and would have
been there longer, had the prison not been forcibly closed.
After an international agreement over Angola demanding the
removal of Cuban troops and their ANC allies from the
region, Quatro was shut down and its remaining 100 or so
detainees moved to Tanzania. It was after this that news
began to trickle out to the world of what had gone on in
Quatro and in Angola.

Documents of this time refer to tribal favouritism among
the ANC in exile. Those in charge in Angola and the first
ANC Government in 1994 were mainly from the Xhosa tribe
(whose members include Nelson Mandela, Oliver Tambo,
and the present President, Thabo Mbeki). Others, like the
Sotho-speakers of Soweto, claim, even now, that undue

privilege is shown these people, especially through greater access to much-prized education.

Speaking of the misguidedness as well as the barbarity of these times, Paul Trewhela says:

'The students were deeply idealistic people. Profoundly influenced by Steve Biko and his ideas of conscientisation, they became the pro-democracy movement within the ANC.

'The violence of the ANC in Angola in the eighties crushed the class of '76, suppressing the pro-democracy movement within its ranks and preventing its flowering.

'It was the students who had the courage to take the extraordinary steps they did on June 16th. For them then to endure years of privation, imprisonment, torture, in the name of the movement they thought was their home was an unspeakable tragedy.

'Yet, they still spoke the truth as they saw it, whatever it cost them. This is what is remarkable about these young people.

'After being released from Quatro and the other prisons in Angola, they were sent to camps in Tanzania where they formed groups of people who continued to ask for democracy and accountability within the ANC.

'They did so at considerable continuing risk to themselves. But they still went public. That is how the world press got to hear about it. That's how I got clear evidence about Quatro for the first time.'

The ANC in exile's version of events was still that it had suppressed unruly mutineers, sell-outs and traitors. To counteract this untruth, the class of '76 sent out their letters.

The one to Mandela in 1990 from the people staying at the YMCA in Nairobi who sign themselves as Ex-ANC Detainees, contains the following:

'It is a fact that the 1984 mutiny was a spontaneous reaction of the overwhelming majority of the MK to crimes and misdeeds, incompatible with the noble and humane ideals of our political objectives . . .

'Had the leadership acted honestly at the very early stages of mutiny and, most of all, had President Tambo responded responsibly to our appeal for his immediate and direct intervention, many lives could have been saved.'

Calling for a full investigation into what went on in Lusaka and Angola this is the letter which asks for 'a commission to inquire into these atrocities' and which addresses the issue of the labelling of loyal ANC people as 'enemy agents':

'Having gone through close to five years without trial in the most notorious prison within the ANC, and having endured the humiliating, dehumanising and hazardous conditions in which some of us perished, we remained committed to the ANC.'

People who sent letters of this kind were not to know that theirs was the evidence on which the need for a commission was put forward, its impetus both to expose apartheid abuses and those practised by the ANC in exile.

Before the Truth and Reconciliation Commission was set up, there were three internal investigations into allegations of ANC torture of its own fighters, the first completed in March 1984. It reports conditions of women personnel being used as 'sex objects', of people being 'severely beaten, kicked, lashed with cables and wires, then half-naked tied to or from trees sometimes for as long as 24 hours.'

Under a heading on Disciplinary Measures the report states: 'some of those punished have been maimed and scarred for life, and there has [sic] even been deaths' and 'Many identify our methods with that of the "boers" and in some cases, feel that we are worse. The aim of the punishment seems to be to destroy, demoralise and humiliate and not correct and build.'

Picking up on the press coverage, Amnesty International investigated and produced a report, released in November 1992, telling of torture by the ANC of its own members over a period of more than a decade.

It details dreadful, systematic torture in Quatro, a man having boiling water poured on his head, people being whipped, beaten and kept in suffocating conditions. The Report's further damning indictment is that the ANC leadership knew what was going on and tried to cover it up.

Following this world interest, two further ANC Inquiries in South Africa were set up and it was then decided these allegations needed to be more formally addressed. Out of this, a proposal for a Truth and Reconciliation Commission, first mooted in 1990, was put to an ANC executive meeting and a vote for the Truth Commission was narrowly won. Years later, when its volumes of findings were produced, the ANC still tried to suppress the specific information of its own abuses.

After wrangles in which the ANC went to court to try and silence findings against them, the Commission's five volumes were eventually handed to President Mandela.

When asked why more South Africans in exile or members of the anti-apartheid movement did not speak up sooner, Paul Trewhela says:

'South African conditions were very polarised. People were rightly horrified by the brutality of apartheid, and they couldn't bear that there was corruption in the anti-apartheid movement too.

'There was also a predisposition not to think ill of an organisation fighting a valiant fight against a terrible adversary like apartheid. And there was, in truth, the difficulty of knowing what was going on in a banned underground organisation.'

He then adds:

'Over here, in the UK, a whole range of commentators didn't want to be accused of being racist. There was that, too. And the channel for influencing opinion, through the media, through various anti-apartheid organisations, did not permit criticism of the ANC.'

These are the conditions in which the youth of '76 became the mutineers of 1984, the so-called 'enemy agents' and 'sell-outs'. As their letters show, they did it for love of their country and the yearning, expressed many times, that it should not be ruled by black tyrants instead of white ones.

Wanting to do their best to achieve their aims, they went public and alerted the world's media. But, unused to handling the press and in fear of forgetting to say something or getting it wrong, they made a decision to write it down. In groups of a handful of people, working from their collective memories, they hand-wrote three almost identical accounts of what had taken place in Lusaka and Angola. One they released to the newspapers, one they kept, the third they managed, with great courage shown by the person who crossed the border with it, to smuggle back into South Africa.

They wanted people there, at home, those who had had to keep their silence for so long, to have the knowledge, first hand: not from newspaper reports, but from individuals in exile who had been known to them in the community and who they could trust.

The person who brought this package back into the country in a suitcase with a false compartment was instructed to give it to one person only. Not to the much revered and trusted figures of Desmond Tutu or Nelson Mandela, but to someone who barely appears in the pages of history – Elias Motsoaledi.

He was a Sotho-speaker and for those who mistrusted the dominance of the Xhosa-speakers, of which Mandela was one, and viewed with concern their control over positions of power, Elias Motsoaledi was the only person in Soweto to entrust with this precious cargo.

Chapter Eighteen

WHERE FREEDOM LIVES

Omry

Soweto, Wednesday 22nd September 2004

The place which bears Elias Motsoaledi's name is the informal settlement, or squatter camp, where Freedom, Andile and Isaac live.

Of the eight men sentenced to life imprisonment in 1964 along with Nelson Mandela, Elias Motsoaledi was one. Which was a shock. Because Elias, a young, working-class trade unionist, was not central to the plots against the apartheid regime on which the trial hinged.

Practically nothing is written down of Elias's life, save his burial in Avalon Cemetery in Soweto, along with people like the young Hector Pieterson, Helen Joseph and Joe Slovo.

Asking Siphiwe about Elias when next we visit the boys and Isaac, he tells us that Elias Motsoaledi is one of their heroes, which is why the community here chose to have their settlement named after him. He can tell us little more, only that Elias was an ordinary man who spent many years in prison for the cause of bringing freedom to South Africa and that, as a humble person, he gave his life to the struggle.

Today we are waiting in Neo's for someone else whose life was deeply affected by and almost taken by the fight against apartheid. I had found Omry Makgoale's name in the cluster of newspaper articles which appeared in the UK in the early nineties, just once. Like Elias he barely appears on the pages of history.

The one reference to him, made by R.W. Johnson, renowned South African author, academic and campaigner, gives a thumbnail sketch of what the class of '76 were up against when they fled South Africa and joined the MK.

The article in a British newspaper tells us that a man, Mr Makgoale, went to school in Soweto with some of the stalwarts of the 1976 Uprising. It goes on to say that he rose quickly through the ranks to become Oliver Tambo's personal bodyguard, but that he, like others, was shocked by what he found in the Command of the ANC in exile.

Eventually resigning his post close to Tambo in protest at the corruption and lack of leadership, he was sent to fight in Angola. There, his obvious personal qualities and the regard in which he was held by men around him, meant he rose swiftly to the position of District Commander.

Trusted by the men around him, when the Mutiny was brewing in 1984, it was to him the rank and file turned to ask to put their case of mistreatment and abuse to the ANC Headquarters. In an attempt to prevent full-scale revolt, he agreed to go back to Lusaka to talk on their behalf. In the process he was arrested on the pretext of being an 'enemy agent' and sent to Quatro.

At the time of writing his article in 1991, Johnson describes this man as languishing 'on a low-level industrial mechanics course in Cologne, desperate to come to England to pursue his studies'. But hopeful perhaps that a new South Africa, with Mandela released from prison the previous year, would recognise and make reparation to men like this, Johnson also writes:

'Watching what happens to Mr Makgoale over the next few months will tell one a great deal about the future of South Africa.

'There are times when one man's life can encapsulate all the dramas and problems of a wider movement, even of a country. Omry Makgoale is such a man.'

Eventually tracking down Omry, or at least turning up an e-mail address for him, he is guarded about talking to me, but agrees to meet when I come to Soweto.

Now, he is walking towards me, through Neo's small green garden, casually yet well dressed in jacket, slacks and open-neck shirt. Gazing from the window, the first thing that crosses my mind is a comment made about the actor Richard Burton when he was young, as looking like a boxer-poet, toughness and sensitivity in one face. This is Omry.

In his late forties, he is fit and supple, moving like a dancer. Although I will learn in a few days' time he does not dance. Around five foot ten, broad-shouldered, slender-to-medium build, it is clear he takes care of himself and his gaze gets the measure of me. When he speaks it is in a quiet, well-modulated voice.

But before we begin talking, he wants to know what *I* already know, what books I have read, what reports and documents I have gathered information from. Used to banning orders in his youth, he is surprised how much information is already published, most of which he is not aware of. He has not read Johnson's article, which I have brought with me.

Omry's Story

Omry was in school at Morris Isaacson with two of the leaders of the uprising, Murphy Morobe and Tsietsi Mashinini, and remembers them both well. Tsietsi's enjoyment of a public platform and his arguing skills made sure the school won top prize in debating competitions. Murphy, a year younger, was calm and thoughtful, his grasp of international affairs setting him apart.

Both Omry and Tsietsi were involved in the Black Drama, Art and Poetry Society, DAPS for short. He remembers

Tsietsi playing Macbeth while he took the two minor roles of the sergeant and porter.

His parents working and, as was common, his grandmother bringing him up, after June 16th, much to the distress of his family, Omry had to flee, not because he was a leader, but because he was close to leaders and from one of the schools which was well organised. Doing well at school at the time of the Uprising and coming from a good home, he was headed for higher education, probably a degree in mathematics.

With no intention of going into the army, he was, however, recruited by the ANC's underground movement before fleeing Soweto, and, along with thousands of others, in batches of four and five people, was smuggled out of the country. Via Swaziland, Mozambique and military training in East Germany, he ended up back in southern Africa, ready to fight.

But in the ANC Headquarters in Lusaka, guarding the ANC President, Oliver Tambo, Omry and people around him swiftly discovered the brutal conditions which were later publicly revealed.

A group of young people, around seventeen of them, decided they were achieving nothing towards toppling apartheid. They opted to be sent, instead, for education through the UN programme, in line with the ANC's promise to young people fleeing the country that they could be sent for an education or be given army training.

This request for education was refused, however, and on

a point of principle over the corruption and lack of accountability at HQ, Omry resigned his privileged position. But on
arrival in Angola, he found conditions there far worse:

'So many people were dying unnecessarily. People were
being beaten to death. It is true the ANC security forces
had been infiltrated by apartheid spies, but people were being
called an enemy agent without proof and being punished and
killed.'

This was made worse by the fact that there were indeed
apartheid infiltrators, both in the rank and file and in the ANC
security forces and no one knew any more whom to trust.

Appalled at the lack of leadership and at the unnecessary
suffering and loss of life, Omry and others called for an
accountable ANC structure through the proper channels.
The soldiers wanted a conference where these things would
be publicly debated and where new ANC leaders in its political wing would be elected to bring the army leaders into
line. This did not happen.

When negotiating for the men, who had refused to surrender their arms to their superiors, Omry remembers saying:
'Look, they don't want to surrender because ANC Security
has been killing and torturing them.'

He did, however, persuade the men to give up their arms,
so long as they were not used against them. They were almost
immediately double-crossed and he and thirty-one others
were imprisoned and seventeen of them taken to Quatro.

Omry speaks of Quatro as a terrible place:

'It was originally a Portuguese coffee farm. Most of the

cells had a concrete floor and roof with low ceiling and a very small window.

'We were taken to a room, stripped naked, thrown to the floor and beaten. The guards stamped on us with their boots, which had nails in them and they were going into our flesh and we were bleeding and screaming.'

Omry was then kept in solitary confinement for eight months.

Like many children in South Africa, Omry spent much of his childhood with his grandmother, Lydia (Mamushi in Sotho). He describes her as a woman who employed 'tough love', an equal mixture of discipline and affection:

'She had tremendous experience of bringing up children. She was very strict and principled, and loving too, so she balanced the warmth and the strictness. One of her sayings to us was: "You can understand everything as long as it's explained to you properly."'

Lydia was an educated person. Having been taught to read and write before Bantu Education came into being, she translated and wrote letters for other elderly women in the community. She was also a good cook. Like many grand-mothers looking after their grandchildren, she made sure Omry was fed as well as educated and he remembers this fondly:

'She always made sure I had a solid meal before going to play. She would often ask if I was still hungry and gave me more food until I was satisfied.'

People of the class of '76 who were at Quatro with Omry say his leadership qualities meant he was singled out for especially brutal treatment. Asked how he survived, Omry returns to Lydia, to the level of childhood care, mentally, emotionally, physically, which built a person who was resistant to Quatro's brutality:

'My conscience was more important than anything. I would debate with myself in my cell: "Was I right in what I did? Was it the right thing?" And my conscience kept on telling me this was the best I could have done under these conditions and, because of it, if I had to die, I wouldn't feel bad about it.'

One of his main sorrows was Lydia's death before his return from exile.

There was one other support for Omry, shared with the other prisoners in Quatro, which the jailors for some reason did not stop. On a Saturday night the men, around 100 of them, would go at dusk to their small windows to sing. They would harmonise, as they were used to doing in the hymns and songs of the townships. And as night fell the sound of this full-voiced choir was eerie, individual voices emerging from different cells in the prison's many low buildings, the combined sound rising and then, caught by a high external wall, dropping deep into the prison courtyard.

On occasion, also from their cell windows, they gave impromptu football match commentaries. Faking a game between two of their favourite teams, Orlando Pirates and Kaizer Chiefs, one of them would pick up the commentary ball, another running with it as that person left off, and another after that. This mock radio broadcast, prisoners cheering as their phantom side scored, was, as Omry describes it, like a precious reminder of something they had all once shared.

When Quatro was forcibly closed in 1988, Omry and his colleagues, still classified as undesirables, were taken by mini-bus to Tanzania and to an ANC holding camp called Dakawa. Only here, too, there was corruption:

'Houses were supposed to be built, and they were not. There was a lot of money not accounted for. So we decided to start work, building the houses, having proper systems.'

Once more, Omry was elected by the people around him to a position of leadership. Which again met with powerful disapproval.

Obvious by his reticent manner that Omry has no wish to revisit those times in exile, either in Quatro or Dakawa, it is from others that I eventually learn the rest of his story.

Many of the young people in Dakawa eventually fled, their lives at risk from that unwillingness to accept the corruption. This is when the three written documents were devised. One group ended up in the YMCA in Kenya, rescued at long distance by the intervention of Archbishop Tutu. This was the group which managed to break the story of Quatro and of conditions in Angola to the press.

However, Omry had had enough. Having been forced to leave South Africa in 1976, he had spent twelve years away from home, nearly five of them in a stifling prison undergoing daily beatings. Exhausted, he decided to stay put in Tanzania and wait for whatever fate had to offer him.

What he could not appreciate was the extraordinary regard

in which he was held by those around him, both fighters and prisoners. People who fled north into Kenya told journalists, and whomever would listen, about this man, a natural leader, an incorruptible person whom the ANC had done terrible things to. Others who fled told the same story, which is how Omry's name came to be a beacon of hope to people he had never met. Unaware of this, he continued his requests for education, to be given a scholarship somewhere overseas. This is what Omry held onto:

'I wanted to study, to use my mind.'

Since killing him may have made him a martyr, the ANC sent him instead for a 'kind of living death', which is how a man who helped rescue him describes Omry's stay in Germany where he was sent in 1990, on a low-grade training course.

Bill McElroy, a primary schoolteacher in London's East End, heard about Omry that year. Initial news of something badly wrong in the ANC had begun to filter through from press reports. As a member of the National Union of Teachers, Bill, like numbers of trade unionists, supported the anti-apartheid movement. It was horrifying news, therefore, to think that there was brutality high up in the ANC in exile, so Bill attended a meeting to find out what was going on.

Convinced by what was presented at the meeting that there was evidence of *systematic* rather than sporadic torture, he joined a human rights committee set up to investigate these atrocities. Learning from class of '76 students, refugees in the UK, that a man called Omry was working on a factory floor in Cologne while wanting to study in the UK, he managed to get a phone number for him.

Through contacts in the trade union and anti-apartheid movements, money was found to bring Omry to the UK. Bill remembers the phonecall and Omry, when asked the question 'What do you want to do in the UK?', replying in careful, measured English:

'Most importantly, Mr McElroy, I want an education. I left South Africa in 1976 and I would have gone to university to study mathematics at that stage.'

'I said: "Okay, but you'll need to sort out qualifications. There are routes for going to university.

'"But the problem is, you're in Germany courtesy of the ANC and you wouldn't legally be allowed into Britain to do that."'

'He said: "What about if I just came?"'

'"You might get arrested and thrown out."'

'"That's a risk I'll have to take. Is there any risk to you?"'

'"No. If they catch us, I'll get round it somehow. As for somewhere to live, you can stay with me till you've sorted yourself out."'

Which is how Omry came to stay with Bill for six months in the small two-bedroom flat in London's East End where Bill still lives. Bill, meanwhile, used his contacts to find a way for Omry to study.

Talking to Bill in the flat he shared with Omry, asking him what it was like to open his home to a stranger, he replies:

'I had no qualms about him. The man is peerless in some ways, his generosity of spirit and his utter commitment to doing what he believes to be right. But this didn't make him easy to live with. We argued a lot about politics and about the fact that I wanted him to see he'd been betrayed by his own kind and he wouldn't have it.

'He wanted to see what happened to him as "accidental" in the sense that it was just individuals or groups of corrupt officials, rather than a corrupt system. I wanted him to see it as it was because I was so angry. And this is the irony, it was *me* who was angry, but he didn't want to discuss any of this. He just wanted to put it behind him and study.

'Omry was like an embodiment of the categorical imperative. And as someone who thought about politics and morality, this intrigued me because it wasn't based on abstract thinking about right and wrong. It was based on a personally held conviction. You couldn't move him from it. He had to do what he thought was right, whatever it cost him, including his life.'

Something of great comfort to Omry emerged in his stormy relationship with Bill, taking him back to sustaining childhood memories:

'He was delighted to be staying with me because he liked my cooking,' Bill says. And Bill, who was divorced by this time, with two daughters away at university and a young son, whom he saw once a week, was only too glad to oblige.

'I was delighted to have my family back, someone to cook

for. I loved cooking and I thought this was terrific. And, of course, Omry hadn't had proper food since 1976!'

It was not long, however, before Bill noticed certain things about Omry:

'Physically, I had to take him to places for sometimes the second, third, time because he couldn't find his way.

'A man of this intelligence would go out into the street, he was going maybe to the supermarket, and he'd turn the wrong way.

'After a while, I spoke to him about it. I said, "You know, you're a trained soldier, you know how to use a compass, you know how to find your way through forests, and you come to a place like this, with the names of the streets and land-marks, and me giving you directions, and you get lost".

'You could see he was baffled by it and hurt. It affected his self-esteem.

'He had been a high-ranking officer and he must have asked himself why it was he didn't recognise buildings and all the other cues anyone would use to find our way some-where. Most of them you're not even conscious of, but you remember the name of a shop, say. And he didn't. So, I recognised that there was massive turmoil in Omry.'

There was also, and still is, slight breathlessness, unusual for a fit man.

'He used to disguise it by standing behind me so I wouldn't see. If we went to a concert he would stand, like children do, just behind my shoulder.

'If you saw his back you might understand all this. The

marks from the beatings are terrible and there's extra bulk around his shoulders from bracing himself and from the damage of being flogged so often, so he stands curled forwards, and maybe this has caused pressure on his chest.'

Bill put Omry in touch with the Medical Foundation for the Care of Victims of Torture and Omry himself tells me he saw a woman there for some months.

But Bill and Omry must have made an odd couple in the time they shared a flat together. Omry, a young, attractive man in his early thirties, a quiet soldier who has been to hell and back, and Bill, twenty years older, a gentle man but carrying a big anger that the atrocities of a white regime in South Africa were seeming to be repeated by an emerging black one. And it was time, in any case, for Omry to move on:

'He needed to look after himself,' Bill says. 'After being institutionalised for fifteen years one way and another, he needed to find out what it was like, not only to study, but go out to the pub, maybe get a girlfriend instead of having me looking after him.

'He moved into this dreadful place near Bow Market. But he didn't seem to notice what it was like. We saw each other from time to time. He would come round here and we'd argue.'

By this time, the arguments were over Omry's determination to go back to South Africa once his studies were finished, something Bill was set against.

When asked why, Bill takes time to respond:

'I believed him to be in danger still, because of his knowledge of the truth and because of his pre-eminence within
that peer group.'

Bill recounts his own version of Omry's Tanzanian trip:
'You know, when they were driven from Quatro to Tanzania,
it was hundreds and hundreds of miles on bad roads . . .'
Here Bill starts shaking with laughter before finishing the
sentence – 'in mini-buses. From Angola, to Tanzania, via
Lusaka – yeah – in a *mini-bus*. Can you imagine it, on those
roads?'

'And when they arrived and Omry tumbled out, what he
saw were hundreds of bedraggled people lying on the ground,
barely able to move, struggling with malaria, malnutrition,
pneumonia, whatever. They were in a desperate state and
when they saw Omry, they all stood up.'

Here, Bill's voice breaks:

'They just couldn't believe it. They couldn't believe this
man was still alive. His reputation for being incorruptible
and courageous had spread far and wide.

'He's such a modest man. He wouldn't tell me this story,
you know. Other people have told me.

'In Tanzania, true to form, within days he was elected to
form a new committee, to clean the place up, make it habit-
able.

'The place was littered with aid workers and all this corruption was going on and supplies just weren't getting to the
people.'

Bill lost his fight to prevent Omry from going back:

'Omry has a deep feeling for the land, pre-modern or what-ever, almost a religious feeling, because of the culture he comes from. So he had to go back to South Africa, to a country where some of those who tortured him would be put into power, given preferential treatment, and others like him would not be.

'He is one of those people you can only describe as a talis-man to those who met him. Stories about Omry will be told by people to their children, to their relations, as the most outstanding man they've ever met.

'His commitment to decent behaviour and standards of ethics is so great that he was a beacon to others.

'That's why they treated him the worst. People who were in Quatro with him told me that every day the guards would shout to him "Come out here," and Omry would never flinch from the whipping, beating, punching. They kept him alive, of course. There's no point in killing someone like that.

Now retired, and still in touch with Omry with Christmas and birthday cards, although they have not met since, Bill says of these times:

'In a way they were the worst times of my life. For every-one in politics here knew what was going on by this stage. We made sure of that. We got the details to the Foreign Office, to our MPs, and nobody, but nobody, in a position of authority stopped it. Or as far as I'm aware, even tried to.

'And it could have been stopped. It only needed someone in authority here to have said to the ANC in exile, who depended upon the West for its support, "Look, we're hearing bad things about you. Clean up your act".

'The tragedy is, if the liberal intelligentsia had behaved differently, we could have got something a lot better. South Africa could have got something a lot better.

'After a while I couldn't cope with it any more. So I said to myself, "Let's just save lives" and that's what I did. We had dozens of them stay over the next year or so.'

Bill was one of hundreds of people who took South African refugees into their homes in places like London, Manchester, Liverpool:

'My daughters got used to it, that whenever they came back from university, there'd be different people staying in the spare room.'

It was these people who told Bill about conditions in Quatro and about other camps and prisons too. It is through them that he heard the fuller version of Omry's story.

Chapter Nineteen

FOOTBALLS

Manoli with footballs

Soweto, Thursday 23rd September 2004

Omry and Manoli get on well together and he is pleased to help her with a mission she is keen to complete quickly. Visiting Motsoaledi on the first day, she had spotted something. No footballs.

Talking to the boys, finding out Andile likes soccer and Freedom rugby, it bothers her that there is nothing for them to play with. Setting herself the task of buying them a ball each and Andile a pair of football boots, she now wants it done.

But buying footballs involves transport to Southgate Mall,

which we do not have. Jabu would take us anywhere at any time but we need to save him for necessary work trips and, cost-wise, Southgate Mall is miles away.

The Mall is also where the quick picture developing service is and I too have a mission. Walking around, notebook and camera in hand, another child in the neighbourhood near Neo, a boy of around eight called Gerald, has befriended me.

We talk daily and, at his request, I have taken pictures of him and his classmates smiling and waving outside their classroom a stone's throw away from our bedroom window. It is from this playground that voices accompany our mornings with their beautifully harmonised singing.

Having taken a picture of Gerald on his own and one of him with me as well as with his schoolmates, he bounds up twice daily wanting to see them. It is no good saying 'I will send them from England', it will have to be a quick-developing job, which means a trip to the Mall.

Our 'proper work', going to schools, museums, offices, homes, we conduct with the patience and dignity you would expect, but this work for children, buying footballs, getting photographs developed, seems urgent and we become merciless in its pursuit. Anyone who offers to pick us up or take us home will end up doing a detour via Southgate. Today, this is Omry, glad to oblige and to be roped into choosing footballs and escorting us round for the morning.

Once at Southgate, Omry looks on in a mixture of awe and trepidation as Manoli gets into her stride.

'But these pictures are for children,' she says in her best pleading Spanish voice, stepping in where my own entreaties to the woman behind the photo counter at Southgate Mall to process the pictures today have failed.

'It is only Thursday morning,' Manoli continues 'and if we pay the extra surely we can have them back by the end of the afternoon.

'The children will be waiting and we have to take the pictures to different places, to Motsoaledi Settlement, to Orlando West.'

Manoli shrugs expressively at this point and, knowing when she is defeated, the woman behind the counter gives in.

Now for the footballs. My job to keep one eye on the car, the other watches with interest as Omry and Manoli survey and test the wares in a specialist sports shop, racks and racks of different size and colour footballs on display. How would they choose? I wonder. But, handling, throwing, discussing as if they were professionals, soon they have a rugby ball for Freedom, a football for Andile and a good, solid pair of size eight boots for him too. Andile is size seven, but they think he will grow fast. I agree.

Freedom's other present to balance up the boots for Andile will come by post from the UK. Seeming to be a natural photographer, his already finished film just handed over to be processed with mine, we have decided to send him Manoli's old camera. I will pack it along with spare films and batteries, and we have told him he will receive it in a few weeks.

But can't I pay for half of today's presents? I ask Manoli. It does not seem fair on her. For which she gives me a very Spanish look. Manoli, I discover, packs a highly assertive eyebrow. Arched in my direction at the moment, it is not to be argued with.

Nor is the idea of lunch for the three of us – Manoli's treat. Accompanying me for most of the interviews I do, Omry's testimony has had a profound effect on her and I enjoy taking a back seat as she talks to him of gentler things: his wife, also called Carol, and two girls.

Omry dropping us back to Neo's after this, Manoli so excited with what she has achieved with the boys' presents, suddenly has a worrying thought:

'Do you think it is a mistake for them to have these footballs?' she asks suddenly over the kitchen table.

'Why?' Neo asks.

'Well, maybe it will attract too much attention to them. Maybe it will make them a target instead of bringing them enjoyment.'

'I think it will bring them friends,' Neo says gently. 'And they are nice boys. They will be looked after in the community.'

Neo then has another thought. 'And just think, the footballs will make many children happy.'

Posing for pictures outside the house, football under one arm, rugby ball under the other, Manoli is a contented woman.

As am I when we go back later for the photographs.

Just as well, for waiting for us anxiously on the side of the road by Neo's is Gerald. I give him the pictures of him standing by himself, one of him with me and the two of him in the group photos of the class. Neo will keep the copies of the group photos, I tell him, and the other children can come for them themselves.

His open radiant smile, as if the world is suddenly all right, is my reward.

Our stay in Soweto is like this, brimful of warmth, work, involvement. Staying at Neo's seems like being at home, only more enjoyable. Here we have warm sun, soft air in the morning, a lovely garden and a choir of voices on our doorstep. We barely step onto the street without people saying hello and callers come to the house too, with material for the book. News of it has moved swiftly round the neighbourhood, what with our local walks, interviews, visits to places like the Museum, and the unusual presence of two white women walking about who are obviously not tourists.

I am moved many times by a stranger arriving quietly with a small package, carefully kept in plastic for many years, a poem written on a bit of torn-off paper, a newspaper article, a letter and, on occasion, parts of an old torn book. I take great care of these offerings, tender reminders of the time when words were precious, banned and, literally, died for.

My thankyou at these times is inadequate but sincere. If Neo is not around, and there is no language between us, I can only smile with my eyes and hold a shyly proffered hand in mine.

We are aware of being protected, though. When Neo has guests for any length of time and can afford it, she pays a group of unemployed young men a few rand to keep an eye out. I had discovered this the day before when walking up the street. Gerald, a big smile on his face, bounding down the hill towards me was stopped, almost in mid-leap, by a loud male voice.

Shouting to a distant figure up the hill that it was okay: 'We know each other', I spend a few minutes chatting to Gerald before going up to find the man who is called Chris. He seems gentle, as it turns out, and had indeed thought Gerald was pestering me: 'The children they do this sometimes, they ask for money,' and he tells me about the other side of life in Soweto.

Aside from the few rand he earns from keeping an eye on visitors, there is no prospect of work for people like Chris. In his mid-twenties, he has never had a job and is not likely to, so he and his two friends eke out what they can protecting people and property.

Most of the problems happen late at night, he tells me, and it is the old story, gangs of youths stealing cars, breaking into houses or attacking people who are out alone.

I feel threatened just once on this visit. In daylight, walking alone back from Tebello's along the Vilakazi, there is a sudden screech of tyres and, as if from nowhere, a white car, mounting the verge, hurtling down the street towards me. The verge banked and wide at this point, I and others are able to move clear. A few people nearby, concerned for my well-being, tell me to stay close in to the garden walls and fences, before we all go our separate ways.

Most people proud of their township and not wishing us to have a bad experience, Sowetans we visit after dark always want to escort us home.

Sometimes caught out by the swiftness with which night falls, we find ourselves out on our own. Walking up the road alone one late afternoon to buy a new phone card, I get caught, first of all, by a long queue at the counter and then, once more, by darkness.

Standing at the traffic lights, night suddenly here, I have a moment of panic. Many people have told us of the on-going violence and, when we ask, the police are described as '50–50'. You might get a good or a bad one. Whichever, they are not on top of the crime, people say.

A man whose son-in-law was killed recently in a hit-and-run incident says the driver and the car he was propelling crazily down the street, in the same manner as the white car which hurtled towards me, were seen mounting the verge by a number of people. But the police tell him it is up to him to produce the evidence. If he produces enough, they may do something.

I put these thoughts away, think instead that Manoli and Neo would send out a search party to rescue me if I was out too long. And cheered, I feel, or think I do, the lightest of touches on my shoulder.

Turning round, there are three grandmothers standing close behind, all strangers to me. Faces so close together, smiling in the dark, they look for an instant like three heads on one body, a friendly triad.

'We are so glad you are here,' they say, almost in unison. 'We are happy to see you.'

So much that is true of Soweto and places like it is almost unsayable, the grief, warmth, fun, humour, hardship, tragedy. I sense that the grandmothers are letting me know I am not really alone here, their form of 'protection'. We stand together for a few moments before, gently extricating my two hands from six of theirs, I head home.

Chapter Twenty

WISHING FOR A GARDEN

Skipper at Inkwenkwezi School

Soweto, Friday 24th September 2004

At last we go to the boys' school, Inkwenkwezi Primary School
in Diepkloof. A mile away from where Freedom and Andile
live, it has almost 600 pupils up to fifteen years of age, equal
numbers of girls and boys.

Here pupils are taught about the '76 Uprising and the
older ones taken to the Hector Pieterson Museum.

'Education is a moral value,' the Headmaster tells us. Preferring
to be called by his nickname, Skipper, he says: 'It is about having
freedom to use your mind and becoming a full, mature person.'

His philosophy, similar to Steve Biko's and Paulo Freire's, is that education is of immense personal and communal worth, combining to produce the thoughtful individuals a strong community needs. He wants everyone to be involved in it therefore, in making sure it happens.

Although for Skipper it is a major issue in people's lives, the harsh reality is that the school does not have the funds for sports facilities or musical instruments and has a queue of children wanting to learn to play.

'This shouldn't be happening.' he says. 'The government is spending millions on copying British school testing systems and this money should be spent on teachers and facilities.

'The authorities are creating a serious problem for this country's future by not educating the children of today or involving their parents.

'I go to the parents and say, "Come to school. We will help you to help your children to learn."'

But people are afraid. Modest also he thinks, believing education is something above them which they do not deserve.

Children chat to Skipper in the playground and the school has an easy-going, energetic atmosphere. He tells us about his plans, for growing their own vegetables in a plot, already dug over, and of involving the children in the planting and growing so that they know how to tend a garden.

But along with being short of funds, there is the added grief of burying children each term from AIDS.

Silence a habit in Soweto, through from the events of 1976 to the refusal to recognise the present pandemic,

Skipper spends much of his time visiting the parents of dead children, trying to get them to face their denial about this illness, saying to them:

'"Look, what do I tell the other children at school? By keeping silent, you are leaving it to me. As a community we have to have the courage to be more up-front about this."'

But, he says: 'People are still afraid and will not speak about it.'

This has a knock-on effect in school, where children have strange ideas about this taboo illness and think there is a monster chasing them. So the teachers have to work with songs, dramas, sketches, posters, to let children know AIDS is an illness, not a curse.

'We tell them, "It is not your fault if you get ill. It is also a good reason for all of us to grow vegetables and to eat healthy food."'

Due to lack of money, pupils have to pay to come to the school, R60 a year, and parents have to be able to afford uniforms. Part of a culture in South Africa signifying a family's commitment to learning, uniforms are also a way of distinguishing children who are at school from those who are not.

Skipper's passion and commitment to the school, its children and the community clearly worn on his sleeve, he has to spend most of his time fund-raising instead of teaching.

'We do not have the resources.' he says simply. 'This is not freedom.'

Talking to people about education and about life in Soweto, this lack of freedom is laid at the door of the present government. In his book, *South Africa*, R.W. Johnson writes:

'Since 1994, crime, unemployment and inequality have all worsened, while the sheer callousness of Thabo Mbeki's regime in the face of the AIDS epidemic and the Zimbabwean tragedy next door have cast a terrible shadow across this early promise.'

The problem with the workings of government is attributed firstly to the voting system. Ironically, this is the much-advocated system of proportional representation (pr). Thought by many to be fairer, South Africans say this *excludes* them from having a voice, because appointments, including at local council level, are made exclusively by the government from a list of people they either wish to advance or owe favours to.

Many commentators write that this has made a mockery of what thousands of black South Africans have died for.

In London, before my visit to Soweto, I speak to John Battersby, previously editor of *The World* and also of the *Independent* in South Africa and now working for the South African government as UK Manager of their International Marketing Council. He is one of many who uses words like 'control' and 'inflexibility' for the present Mbeki Government, but also says:

'One musn't lose sight of the huge headway that has been made. First of all, people's human dignity has been restored and that was, in itself, a massive achievement.

'Secondly, a lot of people who didn't have access to clean running water, something like ten million people, now have and that's an achievement. A lot of people who didn't have electricity now have electricity. And about a million and a half houses have been built.

'What hasn't been achieved is the kind of structural change whereby one could see a closing of the income gap rather than it continuing to widen. In the next five years government needs to reverse that trend because South Africa doesn't have the luxury of a society that can continue with a large gap between the haves and the have nots.

'There's not much you can do with freedom of speech if you haven't got a roof over your head and food and a job.'

Award-winning South African writer André Brink says much the same thing:

'The present regime will not be able to keep international good will and harness the creative talent of its people if it does not change.'

Manoli, Neo and I had headed for a shebeen the night before, Omry having declined an invitation to join us, saying he would be spending the evening with his wife and two daughters and, in any case, he does not dance.

We do not either, as it turns out, the men in the bar being interested in more serious, urgent matters telling us, as Skipper has today, about the problems of living and trying to find work in Soweto.

The words 'freedom' and 'democracy' have followed us since our arrival, rolling round people's mouths almost whenever we get into close conversation.

In continuing conversation over cups of tea and on the phone with Tebello and with Omry, the latter had said gravely how if someone unscrupulous got into power in South Africa, he or she could do devastating things under the present system:

'A bad person could do terrible things to our country.'

Like many, Omry is concerned about the problem the country will face when Mandela dies:

'We must allow ourselves to discuss those problems openly. There must be elections within the ANC. There must be free and fair elections from the ground up and people must be accountable.

'Mandela is a good man in terms of his experience in prison. He managed to reconcile the races but he did not manage to entrench democracy. Mbeki was appointed, not elected. There must be elections and these should be conducted under a secret ballot so that people cannot be intimidated.'

It is chastening to see here, and around us in Soweto, such passion for this one idea which the rest of the world thinks is already in place, 'democracy'. Tebello goes back to June 16th when he speaks of it:

'I used to tell the students that our success is a journey not a destination. What we are seeing now is only the beginning.

'We wanted proper education. After the end of apartheid, we wanted jobs, housing, medical care.

'We are still waiting.'

*   *   *

Neo has lived in the community for decades. My sounding board for talking about local issues and testing out information, Politics with a large P is something she steers clear of. Her brother one of those involved in the uprising and away in exile for fourteen years, they are just glad he came back and the family got on with life.

After his return, their sister, then a doctor, was attacked in Soweto by men at gunpoint looking for drugs. It was not uncommon for this to happen to medical people, Neo says. Her sister, who was heavily pregnant, lost her baby and has given up medicine. She now sells clothes.

To combat the lack of crime control and enterprise money in Soweto, Neo is part of a network of hundreds of 'do-it-yourself' initiatives, people who, faced with no funding, no support, no infrastructure or professional help, set up small businesses themselves.

Soweto is famous for this, its small bands of people and local initiatives. Women form part of the strong entrepreneurial spirit, six of them involved in a 'beading association', marketing their jewellery and ornamented pots. Traditional stokvels still run, groups of neighbouring women putting in money each month to a central pot. In turn, a different woman in the group collects the accumulated pot and with this lump sum buys a second-hand sewing machine, computer, or the lease on a commercial property. If her business grows, she then helps others.

Neo, along with a few local women who are also landladies, is part of such a local group. Between them they have hired a speaker to come and tell them how to manage a B&B and they discuss among themselves how to advertise and pool their resources.

Meeting regularly, they share information, provide moral support for one another and keep an eye out for each other's guests and properties. So it is that if you are staying at Neo's, you will find yourself talking to Pauline when you are out and about. She will know your name, will ask how you are and make sure you feel safe.

The night before, however, coming home from the shebeen early, well before midnight, Neo crossed her invisible, steer-ing-clear-of-Politics line with one telling sentence:

'When the men in the shebeen want to tell the women about democracy and not to dance, you know there is a problem.'

Chapter Twenty-One

High Kicks

Wandie

Soweto, Saturday 25th September 2004

People still coming to Neo's door with precious items, I spend time in the morning making slow haste up the road to the photocopying shop.

A homely shoe-box of a place, high counter, cheerful staff, there is usually room for four or five customers, though not when two of them are standing with their elbows out studying the newspapers and material I have brought with me. Nodding of heads to begin with, comments on the material and interest in what I am doing with it.

Joined by Manoli, walking towards the Museum, in the precinct with its by now familiar open space and stand-alone boulder, a boy of about eight, well-dressed, asks us for money if he sings us a song.

Before we can respond, a woman in her late twenties, walking behind shouts at the boy to leave us alone. Stopping to talk, she tells us how despairing she and other parents are by what tourism has done for this part of Soweto.

'We do not bring our children up to be beggars,' she says, in exasperation. 'Tourism has taught them bad habits. Look, that boy is not hungry.'

As you enter Soweto for the purpose of working on the story of the Uprising, people will quiz you, bring you gifts, tell you family stories, advise you or let you know they do not intend to speak. What they will not do is be indifferent.

With this level of involvement, this trust on your shoulders, you know you will not get it as right as you would like. You will not manage to capture on a flat page the courage, warmth, hospitality, the 'aliveness' as well as the deep enduring silence of this township's people.

Communications from Omry make the point. He wants me to write the best book that has ever been written and I sigh inwardly under the weight of a polite grilling from him over the phone. As well as wanting to know what documents I have read, which archives I have researched, now he wants to test my knowledge of recent history, international affairs and literature too. Have I read Tolstoy, Solzhenitsyn, Dostoevsky, Orwell?

'What did Omry want?' Manoli asks when I hang up.

'He wants me to write the perfect book,' I groan, 'and if I read all that Omry suggests, it will never get written in my lifetime.'

I am on safer ground with our mutual affection for Dickens. Like many teenagers in Soweto, Omry had devoured *Oliver Twist* and *Nicholas Nickleby*. And, perhaps relenting, he rings again later and says how glad he is I am a writer and not an historian.

When asked why he says:

'Because the victims are never in the books of history. They are in the writers' stories. Dickens wrote of a poor boy with ragged clothes called Oliver Twist and historians they write about kings and queens.'

And, as an afterthought: 'Carol [his wife] and I, we have buried ten relatives so far. Five on her side, five on mine.'

As if I would forget, this is AIDS.

In somewhat sombre mood, for this will be our last visit to Motsoaledi, we head off to see the boys. Talking about Freedom the night before, Manoli had said how much she recognised a quality in him which she thinks is not easily taught.

'He stands back, takes things in. That picture he took of Neo, it's beautiful. Neo is herself and he captured her because he waited for that moment.'

Manoli, much taken with Freedom, observes him as he watches others. Seeing in him the 'old soul' which Sue and I do, she is also afraid for him:

'If he has the right help, the right influences in his life, he will make a fine man, but if his intelligence isn't fed, he will not be able to cope with his surroundings or what life has thrown at him.'

Neo is impressed with the boys and gentle with them, I notice. She has a son of her own, Tumelo, in his mid-twenties who, in traditional African fashion lives with his grandmother, Neo's mother, not far away.

Talking of the boys, she thinks Andile is strong and seems practical and outgoing. Freedom, on the other hand, is a dreamer. He misses a mother, Neo says, and is hungry for more than food. She sees, as we all do, the way he is serious and withdrawn to begin with and that it takes him an hour or so to relax. It is clear he needs continuity of a kind none of us can give. What he is being provided with, a guaranteed meal a day and the chance to go to school, seems so slight in terms of the depth of his need.

It is a slim chance and thinking about it as Jabu drives us to the settlement, I wonder if it will be of most use to *him*. My meeting with Freedom having drawn me to help this family, it may be that Andile and Isaac are able to benefit more than he is. I recall again Isaac's phrase about naming a child well bringing a balance of qualities to a family. Will Freedom open the door for his brother and father and not for himself?

Jabu dropping us off at Motsoaledi, the entrance to the small settlement is familiar now and, sadness aside, I look forward to the warm welcome we will find here. The settlement partly hidden from the road, if you did not know it existed, you would drive by the cars abandoned to become rusty skeletons at the side of the Old Potch Road and the empty-looking shacks surounded by trailing barbed wire.

But if you follow the earth path dipping a little towards a vast field you will come across a forest of electricity pylons. They bestride the settlement, children playing football underneath their tall structures, many dozens of them, while the people of Motsoaledi live without electricity.

As we go down the path from the clearing, the place where I first met Freedom a year ago, children stop to show us their makeshift toys or just to talk. It is a busy place once you walk into it. The emptiness of the roadside left behind, here in the settlement a water tap is always on the go, children coming with buckets to fill and women washing clothes in tin tubs.

By the time we get to the Takashana home, they know we are here, Freedom and Andile, footballs twirling in their hands, children milling around, a scene of warmth, friendship, energy. Isaac is here too and comes out, Andile's cleaned football boots in hand, proudly displaying their new shine.

Today Freedom is smiling. After chatting for a bit, I watch the children call to each other and dart around, people coming and going. Leaning against my favourite place, a fencepost at the corner of an empty shack, I stay still, wanting only to capture the scene.

As a child of seven or eight I had a fantasy of putting the

memory of people and places we left behind in our many moves in a tiny bottle, like the perfume my mother carried with her. My way of coping with loss trying to hold onto people when we left, capturing them in a bottle.

Time ticking by, Isaac approaches, and this, too, I would like to capture, the quietness of the way he moves. Wanting to know when I will be back, his hope, partly expressed in the question, is that this is not just a one-off visit.

I can only say 'next year', probably in April, but definitely before the year is out. It is enough, though. A slight squaring of Isaac's shoulders, a straightening of his back and, with his usual dignity, he gives me a nod. Not prone to big gestures, so much is said in an inclination of his head.

A message comes to say Jabu is back waiting for us in the clearing and we must go. The usual handshakes and hugs before we do, Freedom holding on a long while. I say nothing and neither does Freedom as he turns away. Useless with goodbyes, turning to walk back up the track, I call over my shoulder: 'I will be back. I will see you again when I have done my work.'

Subdued in the car on the return journey to Neo's, even Jabu is not his usual ebullient self. But Neo has a treat in store for us. Predicting our forlornness, she is taking us out for afternoon tea. We are going to Rosebank, the place Sue took me to on my first trip back to South Africa last year. Neo dressed up in a glazed cotton black and white dress with matching headpiece, and combative mood, off we set. Driving the car she borrows sometimes from a friend, she keeps up a running commentary under her breath all the way to Jo'burg:

'So you think you own the road do you?

'Typical male driver.'

Neo we discover has a stock of English sayings up her sleeve, delivered in a plummy Chelsea accent.

'Okey, dokey.

'If you've got it, flaunt it.

'Here we are, home again.

'Thank you, so kindly.'

Who taught her these, we ask? Where did she get them from? Neo, who would not tell you a thing she does not want to, laughingly shakes her head.

Over coffee we continue our week-long conversation about life in Soweto, past and present, now and during the Uprising. Neo knew Mbuyisa, the youth in Sam's picture, and his mother Elizabeth, who died earlier on in 2004.

She tells us Elizabeth used to sit outside the church they both attended, Holy Cross, and sell arts and crafts. Unlike her public words in stone outside the Museum, that her son is or *was* not a hero for scooping up Hector in his arms, Elizabeth's private grief was here shared with friends, as Neo recalls her saying:

'If I'd buried my child it would have made sense to me, but I don't know where his bones are.'

The feeling among the women gathered is that the present government has not done enough to help lay this matter to rest, for there are other mothers in this predicament.

Neo says:

'If your child worked for the struggle and nobody assists you in finding your child, that is difficult for you.

'A lot of the children in Orlando West went into exile. But some of them like my brother have come back. After Mandela was released, Mbuyisa's mother was hoping that those who came back could tell where he had disappeared to. And no one could.

'She used to tell tourists what had happened and how no one official had helped her. Sometimes people would say, "She's being unfair to the government", but, as a mother, I understood.

'A lot of people are not saying anything. Some people have been told not to say anything, not to criticise the government. After apartheid a lot of people said we should give this government a chance and not make comments.'

Sitting under shade in the outdoor section of the restaurant, enjoying people thronging by, we notice a young woman sitting at the table next to us. A playwright as it turns out when we talk to her, her husband, a journalist, is at work, her child at school and she is having some time off to think about her new task, writing a novel.

It will be her first and, yes, in reply to a question, it is set in South Africa, in a country and among people she knows. But even so, shaking her head, it is so difficult to bring the words to life, to convey the vibrant colourful ideas in her head onto the page. She is nevertheless intent on the enterprise and, when asked why, replies:

'I have something to tell the books.'

Seeing how serious she is, that this is not a gentle joke, we talk some more and I find I like this notion of 'telling the books'. They have 'told me' for years, kept me up at night with their chattering demands and out of bed first thing in the morning. A fantasy picture comes to mind of books-in-waiting, large empty jackets, rows of them on a shelf having to be patient, on the lookout for a convenient writer to pass by and pick them up, put something in them, bring them to life.

It is what people have been doing in Soweto, I realise. Earnestly, with care in the detail and using me as the messenger, they have been bringing forward their precious material, telling the book.

Back at Neo's just behind nightfall, we dress up, the intention to go out for a last night at a shebeen. Tomorrow, we are having a quiet catch-up day before our return flight on Monday, so we can lie in. But the events of another long day take their toll and we do not want to go out. So, still in our posh frocks, we prepare a simple meal of mango and sundried tomato salad, a bottle of wine from over the road and soon, Brazilian jazz playing, energy returned, it is time to dance.

At some point the phone rings. Manoli and I shimmying and high-kicking round the table, Neo picks it up.

'Jabu,' she purrs, looking up to where we are doing showy sashays and flamboyant turns. 'We are having our own shebeen,' she tells him.

One of Neo's minuscule pauses and then:

'Jabu, if you were a lucky man, you would be here.'

A good while later, and for the last-but-one time on this return journey in Africa, I fall, log-like, into a deep, deep sleep.

Chapter Twenty-Two

NOT AFRAID TO DIE

Freedom, Isaac and Andile

Last day in Soweto, Monday 27th September 2004

The view from Neo's small veranda is familiar by now. Large
cactus bush in the right-hand corner, red bottlebrush, purple
flowers on the yesterday-today-and-tomorrow flowering bush,
the single-storey school over the road with its faded sand-
yellow walls and surrounding wire. In the distance, the Zola
Budd advertising sign, her name in large white letters, legi-
ble perhaps half a mile away in among the highway houses.

Sitting in the cool air at sunrise, bedcover round my shoulders so as not to disturb Manoli by getting dressed, I write

my last notes. Coffee in hand, it has been a ritual of this stay, Manoli and Neo asleep inside, me on the veranda steps at dawn spending an hour writing up the events of the previous day.

I will miss the round-the-table discussions, the family anecdotes and our shared love of food. Neo's grandmother singing, 'Why don't you break the lot?' when they dropped something in the kitchen, or Manoli, as a sixteen-year-old coming in from a long day at the sewing factory. Smelling her mother's cooking at the doorway she is about to exclaim 'Ah my favourite dish' when her mother takes the words from her mouth: 'Yes, your favourite, I know.'

I have felt sometimes the words taken from my mouth or snatched from the page, not because they are favourites, but because they cannot take the weight of saying what is needed of them. Yet words are what I work with and, after ten days in Soweto, the story has stopped tilting. Still with its silent aspects, like music perhaps, gaps between the words which for some will never be spoken.

Playing with thoughts like these in the early morning, I think of Freedom. He is a child who guards his emotions and neither he nor I may ever know fully what they are. Like many, his way of coping is to be contained and I wish for him someone like Omry's grandmother Lydia, who would feed his mind and developing conscience as well as his body. For without the unifying, gathering-together figure of a mother or grandmother, however much Isaac and Andile have stood by him, he will be hungry.

I play next with thoughts of me as a nine-year-old, bigger than Freedom is now at twelve, but also a child under duress, having to change colour in the different homes I fitted into and guarding my hurt. It comes back from time to time, that sense of childhood isolation, of being undefended except by your own skin in an impervious, disregarding world.

I think what a long journey this narrative has been, its beginnings for me as a chameleon of a child, Africa taking root in me as it has in Freedom, making its indelibly solitary and celebratory mark.

I think of Andile. Easy for us all to concentrate on his younger brother, a mark of Andile's stoicism is that this appears not to trouble him. Talking to him, giving him a hug, his calmness is reassuring and the way he looks so like Isaac, indeed well-named as 'the family is flourishing'.

I think of shapes in Soweto, especially vehicles. People still talk of their dread of them, the fear of the dark shapes from the past of hippos, kwela-kwela vans and armoured cars. Military vehicles frequently disguised as white delivery vans, all vehicles were suspect.

Still here, their rusty hulks lie rotting in the sun. What with murders, rapes, arson, knifings, the roadside cemeteries of dead vehicles were a detail in the seventies, and still are. The 'robots' being switched from red to green, year's later, waiting to cross the road, I look all ways round and make a dash for it.

Voices come to mind. Tsietsi speaking in Jon Blair's film: 'We will be what we want to be' and 'Bantu Education taught us to be better tools for the white man.' Children's choir-like singing next; Omry's seriousness; Tebello's defiant passion; a woman called Mercy apologising for her poor English, which is beautiful on the phone; the trio of grandmothers at the traffic lights saying 'We are glad you are here'; the mother outside the Museum; a man called Shadrack, over the road from Neo's, waiting to tell me the history of the community and the Museum itself in deep tones.

A phrase comes to mind from one of the books loaned to me, a compilation of children's writings called *Two Dogs and Freedom*, with the following from an eight-year-old boy:

'When I am old I would like to have a wife and to children a boy and a girl and a big house and to dogs and freedom.'

It is probably eighteen degrees by now, warm soft air bringing the feeling of promise, a good beginning to our last day when an official from the British High Commission in Pretoria will take us for lunch at Wandies.

One of Soweto's old-established restaurants, renowned for lively company and famous visitors, Sue had taken me there the year before, telling me about Wandie on the way. A larger-than-life character who had helped the students in 1976, I hope to find him in.

The restaurant built in the body of a family home and developed over the years into a place which can seat sixty for lunch, inside and out, doubles as a shebeen at night, people coming to drink and dance. After a delicious lunch of ground beef, spinach and pumpkin with jelly and icecream to follow, I find Wandie in his office with ten minutes to spare.

He allowed students to gather here after June 1976. Knowing some of them were on 'Wanted' lists, he let them mingle with other drinkers in the evening. Sometimes as many as ten at a time, it was the only way they could meet.

He got away with it, Wandie says, because it was difficult to raid him with so many people in the bar and, at the first warning of police presence, the students melted away.

It was still dangerous, I say.

Yes, he replies, but it was the end of the line. By this time, being killed for your country was a better option than living with it as it was:

'We came up to the point of "Come what may, if they kill me, I'll be dying for my country."'

One of the many books in my luggage is Nadine Gordimer's *The Essential Gesture*. The Booker-prize-winning novelist and commentator writes of the Uprising that it made people become accustomed to the unthinkable: the continuing deaths of children at the hands of the State.

Examining attempts to appropriate the event, claims from the white regime that the children were mindless criminals and from black activists that the students were ANC inspired and Political with a big P, she observes:

'What neither the accusations of the white government nor the claims of black adult leadership will ever explain is how those children learned, in a morning, to free themselves of the fear of death.'

The phrase 'We were not afraid to die' is used over and again by people who were on the March and those who supported them. Speaking up and saying 'No', was an imperative: 'We were not going to let them take our minds.' Hunger a daily reality and, through Bantu Education, a lifetime of servitude ahead, an existence of this coffin-kind was not worth the candle.

What followed June '76 was, for a while, almost as intolerable.

'It was a long time of violence,' Wandie says. 'It was worst in the eighties when it was crime with political violence and political violence with hooligans.

'It was a mixture of everything, police bribes, sell-outs and the community suffered. People were so confused, especially the youth.'

But things have changed. Wandie is a happy man:

'I feel like a real citizen of my country. I feel like Helen Joseph. I feel like Nelson Mandela. I feel like a President. We are free.'

Leaving Wandies, to go back to Orlando West and then on to the airport for the return flight to London, it is good to know I will be back. Neo asking me the night before over supper if I had got what I wanted from my trip, 'Much more' was my reply.

The memory of her rock-like presence will stay with me, her slow, soft laugh and the fact that she is all there, all here. The opposite of the scourge of constant change and reinvention, Neo is who she is, decades of her, nothing missing, all present and available under one skin.

Jabu driving us towards Jo'burg for the flight, I am pleased that he and Manoli talk amiably so that I can be silent, my mind awhirl: Freedom's face, changing in a week from withdrawn and serious to a boyish smile; Andile's quiet strength; Isaac's dignity; Antoinette's stoicism; and Patricia, who produced fifteen plates of food for the children at Motsoaledi, dancing with two in her hands, a couple up her forearms and one on her head.

Avoiding saying goodbye to Jabu by agreeing we will meet here again next year, I am suddenly aware of not feeling tired at the end of the trip. Our time in Soweto so full and busy, it would be expected, but I find myself instead strangely alert.

Not surprising, then, some time after boarding the 8.30 night flight and settling down, Manoli already dozing by my side, the question flies in. Standing like the Zola Budd billboard in the front of my mind as the aircraft speeds through the night, it will not let me sleep:

'How will I tell the book?'

Chapter Twenty-Three

THE AMASI BIRD

Photographer and subjects

London, October 2004

Sue and I are back to regular e-mailing. Her work in the States and Canada making it impossible for us to meet while I was in Soweto, she is, however, still my main contact with the family in Motsoaledi. To my delight, Freedom begins to phone her regularly, every two or three weeks. Sometimes when Jabu is passing by, he allows him a few minutes of his cellphone time. More often Freedom uses coins in a local call box and Sue phones him back.

Sent: 03 October 2004 7:21
Subject: Re: from Carol in London

Dear Carol,
  What a pleasant surprise. I had a phonecall from Freedom and Isaac on Friday. They were phoning to say thank you and to let me know how happy they were about your visit.

I post Freedom's camera to Motsoaledi, to what Sue e-mails to say, after the event, is probably a residential rather than a postal address. She cannot imagine mail being delivered there.

Sent: 06 October 2004 23:31
Subject: Carol and the address

Dear Sue,
  Oh blast. I've sent, registered post, Manoli's very good second-hand camera, plus 5 reels of extra film and spare batteries, a letter and also Andile's developed pictures.

Sent: 20 October 2004 5:25
Subject: Back from JHB!

```
Hello Carol,
   Isaac has received the parcel for the
boys and everything was in order! They
were so excited when I spoke to them
on the phone. The family are just so
grateful.
```

Having arranged with Sue to increase the standing order to the family from £45 to £50 a month to allow for film developing costs, she and Lennart go to Australia for two months to visit their newly married daughter. They are away for nine weeks from early November till January. Jabu's e-mail on the blink and the occasional phonecall to his mobile producing anodyne information that Freedom, Andile and Isaac are well, it is a long time to be without detailed news.

Carried back from South Africa with me is a book of poetry, *The Return of the Amasi Bird*. Found on the desk of lecturer Jane Starfield on a visit to Vista University, its title is puzzling. This mythical bird is obviously important but no one can tell me what it is.

The poem from which the book takes its title seems to be about education and the Uprising. It tells the story of children who leave a place in the middle of the night, having taken the Amasi bird out of a forbidden pot because 'they'd been hungry / for so long'.

Tracking down one of the book's editors, Professor Tim Couzens, speaking to him on the phone at his home in

Jo'burg, he tells me about the Amasi, or Milk Bird, as it is called. A proverb, written in Sotho, has it that this milk-producing bird is a source of plenty, of the milk of life.

Tim thinks of the poem's title as a return of stolen children to their parents, of the return to a society of its life into the future, its youth.

In real life in 1976, the children stealing away searching for nourishment will be gone for years. They will change into adults, some will die, some will be murdered. All will be away too long. For re-capturing the bird of plenty, bringing mind-food to the children who want it and returning them to their homeland was, and is, expensive:

> We need money
> to buy our birth . . .

> We need money
> to buy our death.

> We have no faith tall enough
> to pluck the stars
> and buy our country . . .

> But we have blood to lose . . .

> from Sacrifice, by Klaus Maphepha
> (*Poets to the People*, 1974)

Along with other distinguished South Africans, the poet Wally Serote is at the British Library in London in October, 2004, as part of a string of UK events to celebrate ten years of democratic elections. The day-long discussion centres on three issues: language, literature and education.

Enjoying the surroundings, the library's spacious twenty-first century glass and red-brick building next to St Pancras station, housing a vast collection of books, papers, documents, Wally Serote asks us first to pause for a moment: 'Stop and listen at the library door, imagine all those writers could speak at the same time.'

We do as he suggests, suddenly aware of the vast treasure in its book-panelled walls. Then he reminds us that only five per-cent-of people in South Africa are readers and, out of that five-per-cent, only half read books. In rural communities, with few books available and so few libraries, this figure will be even lower.

The conversation among panellists reflects how slowly South Africa has moved in enabling children to go to school. Elinor Sisulu, biographer of Walter and Albertina Sisulu, talks about an issue that Skipper, the headmaster of Freedom and Andile's school, spoke of: measurement; and the creeping practice of measuring the wrong thing for the wrong reason.

Skipper's anger was that while children still come to school hungry, the South African Government has imported a highly bureaucratic testing system for primary schools. Viewing this as a smokescreen and a misuse of scarce resources, Skipper's understanding of education is that you feed the whole child, body, heart, mind, not the bureaucrats' appetite to have their boxes ticked.

Elinor Sisulu says much the same thing. While so-called education policy looks for things that can be measured, what about those that can't be, she asks, like if a child is secure or not and able to develop her or his potential?

The name of Steve Biko's mentor, Paulo Freire, comes up next.

As the class of '76 did, Freire argues for education as a crucial component of being human and writes of the power and dignity education *in their own language* confers on people. As he puts it, 'Each man wins back his right to *say his own word*, to *name the world*.'

Thirty years after these words are written, a woman giving evidence to the Truth and Reconciliation Commission shows what a long journey this thought has made, how far these words have travelled.

Describing the personal shame when confronted with a race classification board which ordered her 'to call myself a different thing', she tells how deeply this false label affected her. Calling herself by her true family name is a release from the burden of not speaking the truth.

This need for personal truth in order to live a dignified life makes sense of another of Freire's sayings: 'To speak a true word is to transform the world.'

Gcina Mhlope, award-winning poet, playwright and Edinburgh fringe performer, who has us in thrall with her humour and rich musical voice, gives the conversation about 'truth' another turn.

Talking of her upbringing in a household where respect for other people and knowing about your history was taken seriously, learning the depth of her identity was an important business for her and a long one too. If you wanted to talk about it, you included the ancestors. 'Let's go clean the graves' was the metaphor for having a serious conversation about such things.

She then says something which takes me back a few weeks, to sitting in the sun at Rosebank with Neo and Manoli and talking to the woman having lunch at the table next to us. Gcina says there is a resistance among some people to 'telling the paper', to writing things down, to 'telling the books'. For some people stories still belong on the inside, where they live in freedom, without the threat of being captured and distorted.

A rich oral tradition and a thirst for the kind of truth which was denied for so long – personal identity – leaves many needing stories to be left without interference, inside the mind: Amasi-type food which is not corruptible by outside forces. The integrity of a life, of personal identity, under threat for so long, first by apartheid and now by what Biko called 'Coca-Cola and Hamburger culture' it is only through silence that many feel secure and complete.

But the Amasi Bird *has* come back, and the enduring quality of the March on June 16th shows that it never left. The depth and intricacy of the words used by writers who lived un-peopled in their own country is a testament to the power of language when it is lit from within and a witness for those who stay silent.

June 16th has many legacies, its tragedy and its courageous spirit haunting writers and poets, shaping them to produce highly priced and prized words not just for Soweto and not just for this story but for all those who do not speak.

Chapter Twenty-Four

LIVING FOR A PRINCIPLE

Hector Pieterson Museum

London, October 2004

Tracing the paths of some of the children who rose up in
Soweto and fled to the UK, I find Barney Makgatle who with
Tsietsi Mashinini and another student, Selby Semela, were
called The Three Musketeers by those who looked after them
in London.

Barney describes June 16th as 'a great leap of change. It
turned the tide in South Africa. June 16th ignited everything.

'Where we are today is because of June 16th and this was
planned by students. It was not politically inspired, it was

student-inspired. We were not going to use Afrikaans. We were not going to let them take over our identities and make us think in their language. That is why we marched, to keep our minds.

'When we came to London, the people in the ANC were trying to get us to join them and to say to the media what they wanted us to say. We refused.

'If we joined the ANC it would put the hundreds of students detained back home in jeopardy. If the authorities thought the March was politically organised, they would be asking these students for their ANC contacts, and they wouldn't be able to say them because they did not exist.

'Then the police would be torturing them for information they did not have.'

The first person to offer help to Barney, Tsietsi and Selby when they arrived in this country was the TV producer who made the first film to be taken after the Uprising, the ironically titled, *South Africa – There is No Crisis*. When filming ended in Soweto, this man gave Barney a card. He said if he and Tsietsi ever got to London, to contact him and he would do what he could to help them, which he did.

Jon Blair, a name I recognise. Someone I know well but have not seen for years, it does not surprise me that he was true to his word with the young exiles.

Going to the airport where Barney, Selby and Tsietsi were being held by immigration officials, personally vouching for their identities and character, he got them released and introduced into a system of contacts who helped them with food and accommodation.

The woman Barney lodged with first is Carolyn Clark. Part of a broad grouping of anti-apartheid sympathisers like Bill McElroy and Paul Trewhela, she was one of many people who offered help to exiles until they got on their feet.

Discussing politics with Barney, it was clear she said, that he had little idea what the ANC was until he came to London:

'When the three of them would meet together, what amazed me is how unpolitical they were in a sense. Yet it was a fantastic political stance, with a small 'p', that they had, natural responsive politics, without the context of Left or Right.

'What they had was anger and frustration and moral politics. That made it even more impressive, the absolute bravery of it and, yes, the innocence. I was amazed by the courage of these young people.'

They were *so* young she remembers:

'What struck me, too, was how adaptable, and how small, they were. They were Sotho people, who are not big-boned.

'I was deeply affected and still am to this day, by their bravery and resilience. We know their education had been crap. They were kept down, they were kept ill-informed, yet *their* sense of humanity came out of it and actually won in the end. It was so impressive.' Describing what she means by *their* humanity, she says:

'It's the awareness they had of what is humanly right. Despite the fact you're being told you're less than human and deprived of your rights, you still have that inate sense that this is wrong and you'll stand up and be counted.'

Talking about the legacy of the Uprising, she says:

'It was one of those rare times in history when the people themselves were speaking, not the Politics. Kids that age, you couldn't spin it any other way. It was very powerful.

'Of all the things you get involved in and the endless meetings you go to, to try and sort something, it was helping those kids survive that was probably the best thing I've ever done.'

Abbey Makoe is another person who is clear about the roots of the Uprising: 'The youth had had enough. They were prepared to die.'

Working in the South Africa High Commission with its large windows giving a prime view over Trafalgar Square, he says he is a lucky man to be here. A piece of long luck beginning when, sensing the township unrest in early 1976, his parents who had moved to Soweto to find work, sent him to the countryside when he was fifteen to live with his grandmother.

But like tens of thousands of others, his schooling was held back by the Uprising and its aftermath and he describes himself as living a dozen years or more in a kind of educational vacuum. In the countryside with no qualifications, packing shelves at a small supermarket, by sticking with it he rose to being a clerk. But, as he describes:

'At the end of 1989, I was twenty-eight years old and I was worried that all my chances to be educated had gone.

'Having a clerical job was good by local standards, but I knew my dreams were bigger than that. I was scribbling something on a chart and I found what I wrote was:

'"Of all the things I have lost in my life, I miss my mind the most."'

Reading what he had just written, Abbey handed in his resignation. The political climate beginning to change, Mandela's release imminent, things a little easier, a neighbour paid the R240 for Abbey to do some more studying which eventually led to a thriving career in journalism.

For Abbey, the international importance of June 16th is clear:

'It was a pivotal moment in the history of South Africa. It changed the way the West viewed South Africa and that was very important. We needed people to know the truth.'

The long reach of people's sympathies for what had been done to Soweto's youth managed to help numbers of them start the process of learning. People like Bill McElroy, who helped Omry and many others, Paul Trewhela, and individual teachers and Heads in parts of Europe and in the UK, paved the way for young South Africans to get into schools and colleges around the world. It is what people like Barney, Omry and Tebello had risen up for – the chance of an education.

Chapter Twenty-Five

UBUNTU

Sue and Carol in London

London, January 2005

Freedom and Andile know the story of the Uprising through their lessons at school. Andile and his class visited the Hector Pieterson Museum and it had scared him, he says, to be standing on the place where it all happened.

Freedom is more sanguine about it. Initially saying the event was long ago and he is more concerned about what he can do for his future, later he changes his mind.

Sent: 27 June 2005 14:25
Subject: Re. from Carol re dictionary

  Well, 16th was a quiet day here in South
Africa. Freedom phoned which was rather
special and I asked him to tell me what
was happening. He was very chatty and said
it was a good day to be in Soweto and to
think about the past. The family of the
young man who was photographed carrying
Hector in 1976 [Mbuyisa] were given a lot
of mention because they are putting pressure on the authorities to find out what
happened to their son and brother.
  The sardines are 'running' along our
coast at the moment and it is an amazing
sight with dolphins, sharks, whales and
birds following the fish. So I try and
get to the beach at least once a day.
  lotsa love

For the UK winter and spring months leading up to this e-mail, my sole link with the Takashana family, with Freedom, Andile and Isaac, is Sue. Jabu having had his computer stolen, is still not back on line. Freedom using 'pennies' to speak to Sue on a special deal she has set up, and the cost of calls to me too expensive, I bide my time for first-hand news. Then in late January I have the unexpected pleasure of seeing Sue for an evening during a brief work trip she makes to London.

Having dinner together, catching up, especially with her impressions of the family in Motsoaledi, she speaks of the difference she has noticed in them in the last six months, such as Freedom phoning her on her mobile while she was away. Sitting on an Australian beach she was startled to hear his voice down the line:

'Hello.'

'Is that Freedom?'

'Yes, it is me.'

She is impressed that he rings 'to let us know he's still there' and she talks about the way he has both used and accommodated our coming into his life. Referring to the absence of a female presence, a mother, grandmother or aunt for him to be close to, she says:

'He's making the most of what is available to him.'

Andile is thriving, she notices, and with Isaac she has also noticed a change:

'He comes on the phone occasionally and it's good that he's moved past gratitude. There's an extra strength in his voice. He speaks warmly about the boys, tells me what he has bought for them, what they are doing.'

As Sue is speaking I realise how much I have missed this kind of news and how warmed I am by what she says next:

'What your money has done for the family is to give them back their father. Isaac's sense of dignity has been renewed.

He can feed his children, send them out to play without worrying where the next meal is coming from.

'A father who has a sense of dignity is something terrific for those boys and for all of them as a family.'

While Sue has been away, I have had another thought about the family and the burned windowless shack which is their home. When walking around with Siphiwe that September, he had shown Manoli and me a new dwelling in the Motsoaledi settlement. Although it, too, is made of corrugated iron strips, it has a window and a door and, importantly, a firm concrete base instead of the earth floor which the Takashana family live on. It is also more than double the size.

'How much would something like that cost?' I had asked. 'Two thousand rand (£180),' Siphiwe tells me.

From this the idea takes root and, returning to London, the notion of getting the family re-housed grows. If I managed to raise a bit extra on the price, say £250, to allow for contingencies and some new bedding and household items, it would amount to asking a dozen friends and colleagues to give £20–£25 each.

As it turns out, this figure is way off. Siphiwe has probably counted only the cost of locally bought materials and the bigger cost is employing a contractor to lay the concrete base and erect a good wooden structure for the corrugated pieces to be fixed to. The rest Issac, Freedom and Andile can do themselves, the boys 'buying into' the project and learning to make the home their own.

Discussing money over supper with Sue, she tells me how

important she thinks it is to use financial assistance well from both sides. She believes it can have a destructive downside, making people reliant instead of independent.

Telling me about the family she and her husband have supported for some years, she says she and Lennart have reduced the amount they give because it is becoming a disincentive to the family doing things for themselves:

'We had to say, "Look, we'll help you to create something, a home, an education, an opportunity. But it's not a hand-out."'

I then tell Sue of my idea for a new home for the Takashanas, for Isaac to be more at ease in his advancing years, and a place, too, for the boys to study. Much taken with the idea, Sue says she will investigate it on her next trip to Jo'burg.

We also discuss the possibility of contact between me and the family, both of us agreeing it is better for it to grow naturally than to be imposed. It can probably be instigated on my next trip, which is planned for April, but delayed till September due to work getting in the way.

Sue, meanwhile, will be going to Jo'burg in February and will see how things are on the ground.

```
Sent:      21 February 2005 18:33
Subject:  Weekend visit!
```

```
Hi Carol,
  Well we're back home safely from Jo'burg
and had a 'very special' visit with the
boys and their father.
```

The really sad news is that Isaac has lost his job!!!!!! The Indian lady who owned the petrol station has sold it to the Universal Church who will be building a church and a parking area on the ground. They'll demolish the petrol station and all the staff have lost their jobs. This is the kind of thing that is happening all the time and is just beyond comprehension! Poor Isaac, his shoes were covered in dust as he had walked about 2 hours to get to Southgate Mall where he went looking for work, but nothing.

Andile started High School this year so he needs a new 'blue shirt' uniform and also Isaac had to pay his school fees up front R100 (£9) before he was admitted. I gave him R100 straight away to compensate for the fees he had paid and I'll send R60 (£5.50) to Freedom's school for his fees. Andile's school is Thaba Jabula High School. Freedom will be going there next year.

Both boys look extremely well and my sense is that the family are really 'pulling together' and really are grateful for what we're doing for them. Isaac looks tired, but in fair spirits and determined to do what he can to find another job.

As for the present accommodation, the place they are in is really poor, especially with the boys approaching High School. I spoke to Jabu and he has promised to get some prices for the materials to lay a concrete slab and erect a dwelling a bit bigger with at least one window and a lockable door.

The boys have kept up their writing and like to write about what they have been doing, sometimes they forget.

They were really thrilled to get your fond wishes and send you lots and lots back.

When we left I gave both boys some fruit, sweets and a few Rand so they can keep up the phonecalls from the local box. I discovered that when Freedom phones me it is his own doing. I am impressed with this, as he really does show initiative and a determination to do something for himself.

Sent: 22 February 2005 10:13
Subject: from Carol re your trip

Dear Sue,

Thanks for all the information. It is invaluable you are there.

Considering the awful news of Isaac losing his job, one of my thoughts in hoping to get them moved is to get them nearer the water tap, where people grow vegetables. It's one thought for survival.

I'll deposit an extra £100 in your account to use at your discretion over the next few months. I feel very badly for Isaac. Is there no unemployment benefit for him?

Sent: 27 February 2005 14:22
Subject: Re. from Carol re your trip

Hi Carol,

Sorry for the delay in replying. Have just had a phonecall from Freedom which jolted my sense of guilt.

I've sent R700 (£63) for the family this month.

When speaking to Freedom just now I explained there was a bit extra this month, but they must not expect this amount every month, and he understood.

I'll portion out the rest of the £100 over the next couple of months, depending on how the family manage.

I'm not sure Isaac has any rights to unemployment pay because the people he

worked for were 'sharks' and probably did
not pay the required monthly contributions.
This is a tough country in so many ways.

Looking for a birthday card for Freedom, who will be thirteen on 2nd April, it is difficult to choose. Knowing he has never had a birthday card from London I want it to be something he will like and I have no idea what this might be.

Noticing how many colourful cards show rows of sweets and cakes and pictures of 'the good life', I find a plain card in the end, with a bee-eater on it, one of Africa's many brightly coloured birds.

Sent: 29 March 2005 10:47
Subject: Re: from Carol

Dear Carol,
    Freedom and Isaac phoned yesterday and
had their usual 3 min. chat. They both
sound well and Isaac tells me he will get
a quote on a 2 room 'house' as soon as
possible. Freedom is excited about his
birthday and I told Isaac that I've put
in a bit of extra money this month so he
can do something small for Freedom.

As it turns out, the cost of a new home, with materials, a

contractor for the base and structure, with the family and friends doing the rest themselves, is R6,500, getting on for £600.

It is now autumn in South Africa and they are heading towards winter, which will be cold.

```
Sent:        03 May 2005 08:07
Subject:  Re. from Carol  re Isaac


Hi Carol,
    Freedom phoned on Saturday to say Hi and
to catch up on news. He said it is getting
very cold in Soweto, especially at night,
but they do have clothes to keep them
warm. Isaac is still not working but has
been helping around Motsoaledi in the
vegetable gardens.
```

By this time, the home-for-the-family idea has grown and I am reasonably confident of raising the money. I make thirty copies of a picture of their present burned place along with pictures of Freedom, Andile and Isaac and write a covering letter saying what the project is.

Sue is delighted. Having seen the family recently, she has been careful to put the house idea forward only as a slight possibility. But with Isaac's job gone and, realistically, with him approaching sixty years old, little likelihood of another, it would mean a great deal to them all.

I hope the house we are planning, with two rooms and two windows, will give Isaac purpose, a place to take care of and just to 'be', to stand and gaze out of a window. I think better surroundings will give him the chance to reflect and to find a productive way of engaging his time, even if he cannot find a job.

Sue has been careful to say that the money, if it is possible to raise it, would come from a grouping of people in London and not directly from me. I would not want a feeling of over-indebtedness to skew the tenuous but dignified relationship with Isaac and to interfere with what, in a sense, is one African helping another.

In an old notebook, among my trusted jottings, there is a scribbled page of something said by Archbishop Desmond Tutu on a Radio 4 broadcast in London before the Iringa reunion in 2003 and before the idea for a book.

Listening to him speaking passionately, eloquently, I find myself reaching for a pen to take down his words about something called 'Ubuntu'.

A word I will come across often in Soweto, 'Ubuntu' means 'humanness' or 'being human' and comes about through close relationship.

When recognised and welcomed by other people, Tutu says, we are fully alive in the world, not part of the walking wounded or the living dead:

'I am me because you are you.'

I understand this. It speaks of inter-dependence, of human value being given and received, not bestowed, and of being conducted, not through money, but through who we are to each other.

It is a version of the indelible picture I saw as a child, people being lit up in other people's eyes. You cannot rub them out or close them down. *They* are there because *you* are here to see them.

So it is, Ubuntu in mind, that the prospect of a home for Freedom, Andile and Isaac keeps *me* warm in the sometimes chilly evenings of a variable English spring.

Chapter Twenty-Six

SHOES AND A HOUSE

Isaac and clean shoes

London, summer 2005

The house letters go out in July.

Before I even send them, there is money in the house account. Talking about it over dinner with friends, hands go into wallets on the spot. Clubey – Alan Clube, our maths teacher in Iringa – makes a poster out of the letter and pictures I send him and distributes it round the village in Northamptonshire where he and his wife live. A cheque comes back for £130.

By late July, we know the house is possible. The idea is

for Sue to let Isaac know things look promising and for me
to break the news in full when I see them in September. But
as the money is coming in, a problem emerges with Freedom.

Sue has given my e-mail address to Siphiwe Khumalo, the
guide who took Manoli and me round the settlement and
who now has access to e-mail through a library.

He lives in the next yard to the family at Motsoaledi,
which is why Sue has put us in touch. Contacting me to
help with some spelling, he gives me on-line news of the
family every now and then, mainly letting me know they are
okay. Until, in an e-mail thanking me for my spelling help
there is the following:

```
Sent:        22 July 2005 15:01
Subject:  thanking u
```

hi Carol,
    The other thing i want to tell u is
that Freedom has not been to school since
Tuesday the 19th of July ... I tried to do
some research about that and Freedom tolled
me that he's school shoes are old.

```
Sent:        22 July 2005 17:26
Subject    Re. thanking u
```

Dear Siphiwe,
    I'm glad the spelling revisions arrived

safely, but sad to hear the news of Freedom. When you see him, please say I will put money through for shoes and I will see him in September, arriving on the 15th.

Please will you also tell him I have said it's important for him to take care of his mind and his talents, to learn reading, writing, music, art, sport at school if he can. Maybe there is another reason why he is not going? Anyway, thank you for telling me and I hope he will return to school and be able to learn and be with friends.

I forward all this to Sue.

Sent: 22 July 2005 18:12
Subject: Shoes for Freedom

Dear Sue,

I've forwarded Siphiwe's e-mail, which is self-explanatory. If you think it advis-able, would you please put some 'shoe money' through to Isaac. Or do you think there's something else going on that we don't know about?

Sent: 25 July 2005 13:05
Subject: Re. shoes for Freedom

Dear Carol,

Sorry not to reply before now. I had 'computer burn out' and decided not to open the machine at all over the weekend. I will certainly send extra money for shoes for Freedom. I wonder if that was his motivation for skipping school or if something else is happening at school that is making it difficult. PAUSE!

Just took a break and phoned Siphiwe. He tells me that Freedom is still at home today and that Andile has also stayed at home.

Now that I think about it, Freedom usually phones every second week and I haven't heard from him for a while, around 3 – 4 weeks.

It must be very difficult for the boys to motivate themselves when their father is out of work. I also wonder what he does with his time. Your visit in Sept. will be a good time to see them again.

Sent: 26 July 2005 10:32
Subject   Re. shoes for Freedom

Dear Sue,

Thankyou for putting shoe money through and I'm glad you had a much-deserved break from the screen. We're of the same mind re. the family and, yes, thank heavens for the trip in September.

They may have had a bad winter. Rain comes through their place. The sooner the family knows about the house the better. While I'd like to give them the news myself, they should know straight away. It may cheer them up and it will give them time to think about certain things. Like, for example, if they have to build on the same plot as they are now — a long way away from the water tap — or if they can build nearer.

Sent: 26 July 2005 13:10
Subject   Re. shoes for Freedom

Dear Carol,

Siphiwe is going to phone me back, possibly today, to let me know what is happening with the boys. I will ask him to get Isaac to phone me. I can get a better feel for what is happening if I speak to him myself and will then share the news about a new home.

But Isaac does not phone Sue that day, or the next, or the days after. There are five days of silence. Nothing. And I go through a kaleidoscope of emotions. Why hasn't Isaac phoned Sue? What is going on? What if the family is not up to being helped after all? Sue and I made the checks we could, Sue especially. We have both been to the boys' school, spoken to the Head, spent time in the community where this family lives.

It must be difficult for them to depend on someone they have met only a few times who lives thousands of miles away. What would happen if I got ill, for example? Or if I suddenly stopped the help for any other reason? It cannot be easy for them to believe in their good fortune.

Something else worries me. I have raised over £1,000 for their home. If things go wrong, I will have to return it all. Not until I sent off the request for house funds did I realise how heartfelt people's responses would be, letters with messages, like: 'What a wonderful thing to be doing'; 'What a great project'; 'Thank you so much for asking us. We would hate to have been left out'; 'Do you need help with the building work? I'm serious. Would love to meet Isaac and the boys.' What would I say to the people who had sent money and these messages in good faith and in such good spirits?

Friends are marvellous as always. Tuesday when I last heard from Sue, by Sunday I crack.

'It will be something small,' Gordon says when I phone him on Sunday afternoon with my tale of anxiety and woe.

On Monday morning at last a message from Sue. The boys

had phoned her, were apologetic about not going to school, but their needs seem genuine. And Sue and I in our busy lives had missed a few things.

She had written in May that Andile was asking for an English dictionary. This request had been shelved, taken over by the house project. As was one that Isaac made to me almost a year ago. He had mentioned Andile would be going to High School and needing a blazer. In everything that was going on, I forgot about it.

```
Sent:      01 August 2005 07:20
Subject    Re. from Carol
```

Dear Carol,

   On Saturday I had a phonecall from Andile and Freedom. It seems the boys were skipping school because they both had bad colds and wanted to try and make some money [a few rand from odd jobs or begging] for the items that they needed for school. For Freedom it was shoes which have now been purchased so he will be back in school today.

   For Andile it is a slightly longer list. He requires an atlas, an Oxford School Dictionary, a geometry set and a school blazer. Once purchased they will hopefully last them for their time in High School.

The blazer can be passed down to Freedom.

Isaac phoned yesterday morning. He has been quite ill with flu. He was on his way to buy the shoes with Freedom and phoned from the shopping mall. I told him about the house, as you suggested. I wish you could have heard his reaction. He was speechless, just so grateful and very emotional. I am sure that not having a job and trying to provide for his 2 boys weighs heavily on him. He is a proud father, a proud man who is just trying to make ends meet in circumstances that are difficult.

Sent: 01 August 2005 10:56
Subject: Re. from Carol

Well, what a relief to hear from you. I somehow feared they were going through dark times. It must be dispiriting for Isaac to have no structure. I am just glad they all now have the house news to lift them. And you and I will see each other in seven weeks!

Chapter Twenty-Seven

RETURN TO SOWETO

The boulder: words on stone

Soweto, Thursday 15th September 2005

Manoli not with me on this trip to Soweto, she has returned to live in Spain after our trip to South Africa last year and I will miss her company and enthusiasm.

This time though, I know where I am going and have pictures in mind of the people who live here. I am eager to see Freedom, Andile and Isaac again, Neo, Siphiwe, Omry and Tebello, and to be joined by Sue for a few days. I am looking forward to revisiting the Museum, where I will spend some time sitting in the grounds.

The bad news is delivered within ten minutes of arriving back on African soil. Having met me early at the airport, driving towards Neo's, Jabu turns and says: 'Things are not good with the family in Motsoaledi. Freedom is not at school and there is a problem with Isaac.' Drinking is involved and the boys are not telling anyone what is wrong.

My spirits plummet. Sue had mentioned Isaac looking tired, but nothing more. What can have happened? How are the boys? Have they been harmed? Will I be able to help? How long have things been bad?

Dropping me off at the Vilakazi, Jabu saying he will come back in a few hours to take me to Motsoaledi, the sound of a special greeting through Neo's open windows, the Brazilian jazz Manoli and I danced to on a Saturday night last year, is lost on me.

Neo's hug is not. A warm welcome, a sit-down at the table with a cup of tea. Neo eager for news of Manoli, I tell her she is busy looking for premises to set up an Alexander teaching centre in Barcelona and looking forward to hearing news of this trip. Eventually I tell Neo about the problems with the family.

Knowing so little at this stage, I can only say what I have been told. Neo nods her head. She has heard this before and unfortunately it happens a lot. Squatter camps can be terrible places to live: rats, crime, poverty, disease, violence. Drink is always an enticement in these circumstances and the boys are at an age when they need the discipline of a

father. 'You must see for yourself,' she finishes with. 'Then
you will be able to judge.'

Jabu driving me over to Motsoaledi, I seek out Siphiwe
again and gather as much information as I can from him and
from Jabu and his long-term driver Leclela who comes along
from time to time.

The consensus is that Isaac, being unemployed and having
failed to get another job, has fallen into bad company where
people are drinking. It is a worrying feature of the camps,
groups of men sitting around with nothing to do. In the last
six months, Isaac has stopped taking care of the boys and
they are dirty. However, they will not tell Siphiwe or Jabu
what is happening in the home and why Freedom is often
not in school. They have clammed up.

Leaving Jabu, Siphiwe and Leclela at the top of the road,
wearily, I head down.

Out of respect, it is important to talk to Isaac by himself.
I am a woman, he an older man and I want to be careful
that he does not lose dignity.

The dirt yard is different this time. Deserted, no other
children, like a painting stripped of colour, an old wooden
bench knocked over, a piece of brown tin laid diagonally
across the entrance to the Takashana house blocks the way.

But there is something else different here and remarkable
– Freedom. He is expecting me this time and as I round the
corner he and Andile are waiting together and Freedom looks
at me with a long deep gaze that is brimful with recognition.
The same height and weight, still looking nine years old, his

eyes have changed, expressing not guardedness but deep pleasure. No longer the held-back child of last year, he smiles at me warmly, openly, as if we have known each other for years.

Andile, too, has changed. Now fifteen, the elder brother we thought was calm and confident is not any more the stronger child. For the moment, at least, he has lost some ground. He has dropped weight, is not thin, but slender, as Freedom is. In a little while it will be he, not Freedom, who will say to me, walking back up the road, 'I have missed you, Carol.'

For now, warmly we exchange greetings. I have not let them down, their happy faces seem to express. I am here, back again, my exclamations of 'I am so glad to see you both' delightfully received, but not I notice my instinct to give them a hug. It is clearly not what either of them wants this year.

Now though, the person I am anxious about, Isaac, emerges from inside the dark house, from behind the tin boundary and he too is very changed. While clearly not drunk, he is jangled, strangely excitable, the manifest stillness of last year replaced by jerky jack-in-the-box movements. Like Andile, he is thinner and I have an impression of him being much shorter, which he is not, but a loss of stature makes it seem that way.

Struggling to capture the changes in him, I take inner snapshots, a habit from childhood.

The overall impression is that Isaac is dirty: dust on his

shoes; baggy grey trousers scuffed; his face wizened and he unwashed and dishevelled as he struggles to tighten his belt. That is the semblance, except for the shirt which I do not notice till later with my mind's eye. It is spotless, white with a smart thin maroon stripe, neat cuffs, newly pressed.

Beginning by saying I am glad to see him again, he and I both know my heart is not in it. I want to say: 'What is happening here? What is going on?'

Replying equally cautiously that he is glad to see me, the four of us stand for a moment or two, Freedom, small but strong by my left side, Isaac in front of me, Andile, more hesitant, off to Isaac's left, my right, all a few feet from each other.

'May I take the boys to tea tomorrow?' I ask as a way of saying something simple and what I believe to be uncontentious. I am wrong.

'You can take that one,' Isaac says pointing at Andile, 'but not this one,' pointing to Freedom.

Alarmed by the crudeness with which he calls his children 'this' and 'that' and trying to grapple with what Isaac is getting at, I notice the boys look uncomfortable, turning away from me, heads down.

Then a crazy story starts, in its first words the main clue to its unravelling: 'I have a job,' Isaac exclaims, pointing at himself, as if he is a child. 'From today I have a job,' he repeats, with great excitement.

This is not the case. Nor is most of what follows, although I will come to understand some of what Isaac says and why it besets him.

The story he tells is that the family is under threat. People are saying they will kidnap the boys who have a police escort to school every day because of this and a helicopter is coming to take them all away to safety this very afternoon, Isaac says, pointing first at the air and then at the ground. The helicopter will pick up Freedom first, which is why he must stay and, by this afternoon, they will all be gone.

This is crazed talk, and feeling helpless I try and address it a different way: 'But I have travelled five and a half thousand miles, a long way from across the world, to see you and your boys,' I say. 'What if you were gone when I arrived. How would I feel?'

Isaac says he would have left a phone number with someone, although he cannot say who.

That Isaac has been more than a good father shows in the calibre of his sons, in some of the small things they say and do in our next few days together. They are boys to be proud of. Isaac, their sole guardian since they were small, must take a large share of the credit for this. But Isaac, for now, seems to be gone from himself and unreachable.

Walking down the road with him, so as not to be overheard, I come to the point: 'Isaac, it saddens me to see you not yourself.' When there is no answer to this, I say: 'I have heard you have been drinking.'

Isaac says that bad people must be telling me this. My answer that good people who are concerned about him and the boys are worried about them cuts no ice. Isaac insists he is not drinking and puts the problem onto people who are trying to kill him. He tells me he barely sleeps at night for fear of the threat to his and his boys' lives.

This is too much to make sense of for now. I have no idea whether this is based in reality, paranoia or a bit of both. Walking back to the yard, I resume the subject of taking the boys to Neo's for tea.

Isaac still insisting I can only take Andile, it is Freedom who chimes in, talking to his father politely in Xhosa, but speaking as a younger adult, not as a child. Isaac demurs, Freedom says something else and looks at me: 'You can come for us tomorrow. In the morning. Come early. Nine o'clock.' This is said clearly. A big change in Freedom and Andile is their much-improved English.

Walking back up the red earth road, Siphiwe, Jabu and Leclela are waiting for me. All these men are fathers, Siphiwe in his twenties, Jabu in his thirties and Leclela in his forties. I tell them I think it may be more than drink with Isaac, unless he has taken some bad drink which has done something to his mind.

I tell them the story of the alleged death threats, the police escort and the helicopter. With the first, they say there has been trouble in a few of the yards, but that the company Isaac keeps is 'bad for his head' which feeds on rumours. The police escort is simply not true and I know the helicopter is a sign of Isaac's desperation to escape whatever troubles him.

But shocked by the change in him and worried for the boys I am suddenly tearful: 'What if he takes them away this afternoon? What if they are gone?'

That will not happen they tell me and the three of them begin to do something very African. They talk around the subject, encircling it, Leclela's voice the most poignant.

Saying that Isaac is a man who has loved his children, who still does, but the love cannot come through, we must find a way to see if we can let this happen again he says. The three of them encompass, too, the crucial question of the absent mother-figure. Isaac has managed so long on his own without a woman's help. Suddenly, after losing his job, it has become too much.

There is talk of Isaac being afraid of having his boys taken from him. Not rational in a part of the world where over-stretched social services are thin on the ground, but the fear arising from the terrible blow of sudden unemployment coming at the same time as his advancing years, Isaac feels less of a man, and so less of a father, and is afraid he will not be allowed to be one.

But the important thing is that the boys must speak. They must talk now, while they are young, before they grow older and seal up what is in their hearts. I can do that. They will talk to a woman.

It is perhaps good that this is the day Jabu and Leclela take me to Avalon Cemetery nearby. So much a part of Soweto's history, so many of the class of '76 buried here, it is a place to shed tears for the hardship of this community, for the lives lost then and for people like Isaac, all at sea now.

In my mind I had thought perhaps there were hundreds

of graves here, but there are thousands in this vast, almost treeless expanse. More than ten thousand perhaps, which is why the gated grounds are ringed by vehicle tracks. With the temperature at 35 degrees, you would exhaust yourself from going on foot. Airless and sprawling, even head-high tombstones are flattened by the heat haze and distance.

Inside the gate, on the left is a stand-alone momument to the class of '76: slender brick columns with a roof over a marble coffin-sized slab, tilted for what is inscribed on it to be read.

Called the 'Never, Never Again Monument' words by people's poet Mzwakle Mbuli, begin with: 'Young people of this land, you are amazing . . .'

On Hector Pieterson's headstone, his full name, Zolile Hector Pietersen (spelled with an 'e' here), the dates of his life August 19 1963, June 16 1976 and the words:

'Time is on the side of the oppressed today. Truth is on the side of the oppressed today.'

Jabu thinks we will not find a grave I am especially looking for, but almost next to the monument for Tsietsie (with a final 'e') Mashinini, Jabu suddenly gestures to the simple grave of Elias Mathope Motsoaledi. Almost seventy when he died, the headstone bears only the words: 'Remembered by his family RIP.'

Leclela driven on, Jabu standing by, I think of Elias's twenty-six years in prison and of something Omry has told me of the fatherly quality in this man. A slightly built person, he visited some of them in Tanzania after receiving the smuggled document. 'We know this,' Elias had said about the damning evidence in it and, as if to protect Omry and the others from further acts which might cost them dearly: 'Take my advice. Keep quiet for now. You are young. Save your lives.'

Dusk by the time we return to Neo's, my red eyes telling of many tears, suddenly I feel guilty. Manoli and I were a double act last year, her delight at being in Africa taking up the slack when my mind was occupied with work. She filled in the gaps, kept the social momentum going and I miss her liveliness and support at the end of this disturbing day.

Lying on the bed, my mind wanders around. What has produced the difference in Isaac in a year? Is there some kind of cultism involved in Isaac's dread and paranoia? Driving me from the airport this morning, pointing out changes since last year, Jabu had mentioned a sudden influx into the region of evangelicals. They have come en masse, he says, many over the border from Zimbabwe, and are building vast tents to hold meetings to 'rob the poor'.

Is this the reason why Isaac is now a fearful man, his repeating, over and over 'as God is my witness'? Has the arrival of a small amount of money produced this problem? Will the house help, or will it make things worse?

But not all has gone wrong. The boys are still fed and, as Freedom and Andile will confirm tomorrow, they are given their R2 (18p) to go to school. Drink is a factor, but it is not the only one.

Then my inner camera rests on what I would have

forgotten without it, Isaac's shirt, his attempt at a fine and proper greeting. And his first revealing words: 'I have a job. From today, I have a job.'

I recall the way he spoke about work last year. The people running the garage paying only a third of the national wage, nevertheless Isaac loved his job because, he said, he was the grandfather. An intelligent man, and discursive, able to ponder and to enjoy thinking around a problem, many people came to him for advice. His experience as an older man was made use of, and he had standing in this roadside business community of travellers, regular customers and passing cars.

From the outside a lowly petrol attendant paid a meagre wage, but he made the job his own, my clear initial picture of Isaac one of personal pride and orderliness. Up early to get the boys to school, working five and a half days a week, on Saturday afternoon the weekly washing was done, Sunday, his day off, he was at church with his sons. It was a disciplined life.

When the job went it was probably clear after a few months of getting dust on his well-polished shoes, he was not going to find another. At the time when he loses his place in the outside world and his status, his sons are gaining ground. It is as far as I get for now.

Calm and considerate as she is, I sense Neo is waiting for me to rouse myself. And I do. A quick change, on with a sequinned top, earrings, bracelet, splash of perfume and I join her in the kitchen to prepare a meal and keep her company as Manoli and I did last year.

'Okay, I'm ready for the jazz now.'

Chapter Twenty-Eight

THE HEART OF THE MATTER

Girls in the Settlement

Soweto, Friday 16th September 2005

Sitting on the step in the morning, the Zola Budd sign has gone, replaced by something green-coloured which cannot be read from this distance. But the children's voices from the school opposite, the powerful scent of yesterday-today-and-tomorrow lilac and white blooms are here. 7 am. Another day.

Chatting to Neo last night, returning to talking about the family, I had asked her opinion about the house for Isaac and the boys. The problem is that the money for it does not come from me, I tell her, and I feel the need to show it has been well spent. If it were my choice, the house would be built tomorrow, but I must be careful. What does she think?

Neo spends time before answering and speaks slowly when she does. The boys do not deserve their father to be unwell and they need a place to study. It is the only way for them to get a better life. There are people in the community who will tell me what is going on and they too will help the boys. The house will give Freedom and Andile a chance and maybe it will help Isaac too. They should have it.

The house is in the front of my mind this morning because of something Jabu has said. He visits squatter camps regularly, taking people like Sue and me who he thinks might make a difference, not just to Motsoaledi but to the other settlements nearby. Yet accustomed as he is to poverty his comment on visiting the Takashana home is: 'No one should have to live in a place like that.'

Having kept quiet about it while it is all the family has, I know I would not survive a week in it, maybe not a weekend. Sticking my head in this time in the middle of the day, the heat nearly overwhelms me, along with the sudden overpowering darkness.

The floor space almost completely taken with three single beds, two pushed together at the back for the boys, who climb over one to get to the other, and one abutting which takes up the rest of the length as far as the hole for the door, there is room only for three people to stand up in the remaining space.

The wall opposite the door taken up with a primus stove and a cupboard, a tin bath for washing and bathing kept outside, it has taken extraordinary stores of discipline, ingenuity and vitality to live here. Perhaps not surprising that Isaac with only this to look forward to all day, has caved in.

But life in the clearing at Motsoaledi on a lovely Friday morning is not without moments of humour. Andile, waiting for us just before nine, goes down the track to fetch Freedom. Gone around ten minutes, Freedom comes back up the track, but now we are missing Andile. Another ten minutes and a boy is despatched to see where he is. He reports that Andile is in the house and not coming out. Thinking this routine might go on all day, I go down.

Andile, coming out of the house as I come into the yard, is ill-at-ease and, as I touch his shoulder, I find out why. His shirt is damp and suddenly I understand. No clean clothes to wear, not wanting to come out in dirty ones, he has tried to clean these while standing up in them. He and they are wet and, on his feet, he is wearing old blue carpet slippers. Children forbidden to wear school shoes for play so as to keep them for best and to make them last, it is out-of-school shoes he does not have as it turns out.

'I am sorry to keep you waiting,' Andile says in obvious distress and impeccable English.

'I know things are difficult,' I reply, telling him not to worry.

Both boys wearing the orange socks I brought off the plane yesterday are a motley sight: Andile in damp T-shirt, grey pedalpushers and blue slippers; Freedom in a grey bomber jacket many sizes too big, brown shorts and striped plastic shoes.

Isaac is nowhere to be seen. He has gone to a traditional healer, Freedom tells me, pointing far away through the line of pylons stretching up over the rise. Before we go, Siphiwe makes us stop for a picture, Andile ill-at-ease, me my usual camera-shy self, only Freedom looking pleased with life.

The boys have not had breakfast, although they do not say this until asked. Stopping at a roadside stall on the way back to Neo's, Jabu tells me fatcakes are the answer: dough cooked in fat, like a jam doughnut but without the jam. Buying a dozen or so, a couple for Jabu and Leclela too, sitting with me in the back of the car, hungrily the boys tuck in.

A short while later under the shade of an open wooden gazebo in her back garden, Neo lays out more food: bread and butter; cake for afters and plenty of juice. Sitting at one end of the large garden table, me at the other, Freedom and Andile on either side, Neo looks on, listening, but not needing to interpret because the boys' improved English means they can speak for themselves this year.

Their story is swiftly told with only slight prompting. A short while back Isaac stopped cooking and cleaning. Since then they cook for themselves and do the washing and ironing. Or not, as seems to be the case.

Although they do not use these words, it is clear they lack structure and the presence of what they had last year when they looked so different, Isaac's organising hand.

Food is still bought for the household, the three of them going together to the local shop. It is just that Isaac does

not help them any more in preparing it, in cooking and washing up.

'When did the problems in the home begin?'

The boys are specific. Four months ago. In May Isaac told
them he had problems with his heart and could not do things
any more.

Afterwards I wonder if Isaac meant emotional problems
with his heart, whether he meant physical ones, or both.

'And the other problems?' I ask Freedom and Andile.

After that Isaac has told them someone has been hired to
kidnap one of them and they are both afraid and this is why
Freedom is not in school.

My heart sinks again. This is so difficult to deal with. I
have spoken to Freedom's class teacher, Charles Radzilani,
on the phone, who tells me that Isaac does not get Freedom
up in the morning any more. He says Freedom is an especially bright child and it is frustrating that even when he is
at school, he falls asleep at his desk.

My hunch, confirmed later, is that there are children
nearby whose parents have managed to tap into some free
electricity for TV and, Isaac having lost control, Freedom
stays out late watching.

Moving between letting the boys know I will help them
and being clear they are not going to be allowed to get away
with things, I ask Freedom if he stays away from school to
beg money from tourists. Hesitating, he replies that other boys
he is with do this. So a yes then, Freedom using his able mind
and conscience to think of a way of not telling a lie.

Freedom himself then volunteers that Isaac is drinking and the statement: 'My father is too old to drink.' When asked if he can say how much Isaac drinks, he immediately replies 'Twenty per cent.'

I am not sure if he means twenty-per-cent of the time, twenty-per-cent of the money, or if he is doing something not unusual in these parts, keeping me happy by answering when he hasn't got a clue. People do this a lot. Trying to respect – or confound! – the Western question-and-answer mode, they do their best to satisfy or subvert it.

Letting them know I am concerned about their difficulties, I ask Andile what he thinks I could do for them which would help most.

Speaking softly, almost in my ear, he says: 'The house. Having the house.'

Having the house will make life better for him? I half ask. He nods. And seeing how uncomfortable he is, sitting in damp clothes, I do not ask more. Obviously it will be easier for him to take care of himself if he has room to wash, to put things away when they are clean and to have the relief of light, space and a room of their own.

However, when asked what would make his life easier, Freedom replies, quick as a flash, 'a television'. On form, his new-found confidence showing, he looks spry when he says this as if he knows he is chancing it.

'No way,' I say, with mock severity, but conviction. 'You are not having a TV until you have passed your exams, probably in three years. I am not going to get a TV for you to stay away from school all day watching it instead of studying.'

Full of surprises today, Freedom rewards me with a beaming smile. 'These are the words of a serious person,' his expression says, 'someone who will look after me.'

He looks both cool and mis-matched in his too-big bomber jacket, shorts and plastic shoes as we wander out onto the street to see Mandela's house, which they missed last year. Freedom is excited, chattering away as we walk up the road.

A number of school parties already here in the small one-bedroomed house, and more waiting to go in, there is barely room to stand. We spend the longest time in the bedroom looking at the animal skins on Mandela's bed, family pictures, mementoes, and Mandela's old boots and shoes under a shelf by the window.

On the way out, noticing the shop in the yard is empty at the moment, I suggest going in, but they shake their heads. As I will find out on Monday, their sharp-eyed way of clocking prices and adding things up in their heads, has already spotted the entry fee: it amounts to R40 (£3.60) and they do not want me to spend any more.

Talking on the walk back down the hill, Freedom, it turns out is a good swimmer, loves the water and it is he who speaks more than Andile, asking me questions about the sea. He has only swum in a pool. Is the sea all around the UK? he wants to know. And what does it feel like? Does the water keep you up? How cold is it?

They tell me about a school trip in a coach to Pretoria Zoo, around an hour away. It is the furthest they have been from Soweto and they were both excited by it. Andile liked the travelling, being in the coach and looking around at his surroundings. Freedom took pictures of the animals, which he would like to show me, but he is not sure where they are. I tell him I will see them another time.

Buying more food on the way to give them something to eat when they get home, I see Andile put a big-brother arm round Freedom's shoulder. Nonchalantly, Freedom shrugs it off.

The boys' courtesy is clear as we are out and about, the way they wait for me to go first, stand aside at each room in the Museum until invited to go in and, as we go back, Andile takes the large bunch of keys from me when I am struggling to find the one which opens Neo's gate. Having watched me use them as we came in earlier, straight away he picks the right one of more than half a dozen, opens the gate, locks it again and hands the bunch back to me.

But before we part for the day, another small exchange, a step in the beginning relationship we have together. 'I got your card on my birthday,' Freedom tells me with great pleasure.

Glad that the picture of the bee-eater, sent five and a half months ago, hit the spot, I ask what about Andile's? I sent him one too, his birthday a month later, at the beginning of May.

Andile looks awkward. Did it not arrive? He shakes his head. Letting him know it was sent, that I would not leave him out, I make a mental note: when Sue arrives and we take them shopping on Monday, buy Andile a replacement birthday card.

Chapter Twenty-Nine

THE RESTAURANT BUSINESS

Freedom, 2005

Soweto, later on Friday 16th September 2005

Having won a Township Accommodation award for the second year running, Neo is alert for an inspector calling at any time and would not like him to see what I have made of her tidy rooms. Without Manoli to consider, my files, address books, notebooks, hat, camera, diary, water bottles, sweets for the children, pens are scattered all over the spare bed which Sue will occupy on Sunday night.

Going in for a shower, I hear Neo's broom on the soft honey-brown tiles outside, sweeping towards me. Like Mma

Ramotswe in Alexander McCall Smith's *The No. 1 Ladies'
Detective Agency*, she wants to make sure she keeps her
plaque for excellence without me getting her down-graded.

Shower over, I am about to untidy the pristine bedcover
by lying down to read but, missing a glass of water, pad out
to the kitchen.

Which is where I find Freedom, standing outside the door
on the verandah. Neo, looking disconcerted, has just let him
in the garden gate and is wondering what to do.

Freedom having walked three miles to spend the rest of
the afternoon with me is looking doubtful now, worried I
might be angry with him. Seeming very small and young
again, 'I have come to see you Carol' is what he says. Andile,
as it turns out, is playing football.

He has brought two even smaller friends along for
company, a child whose Zulu name, Xolani, I cannot easily
pronounce so I use the English translation, Peace, and his
other friend, Pule (pronounced Poollay and meaning rain)
who are both eleven.

Well, all right, I smile at them, a first thought being are
they hungry? – a nod of their heads – and a second that Neo
has had enough invasions for one day, so we will go straight
to the Hector Pieterson Museum for what will be their first
visit.

Neo telling me where to buy 'kotas' on the walk up, the
word brings big smiles from my young charges.

A version of chip butties as it turns out: a large bap, chips,
cheese and plenty of tomato sauce inbetween. Buying them

from a food-stall up the road, I call Freedom into the small trailer, jacked up off the ground, where a fridge is stocked with cold drinks. His eyes go to the drink he had at Neo's this morning, but he chooses something else. When asked why, he says he thinks the first one is too expensive. The difference being only a few rand, I tell him they can have it for today as a special treat.

Peace and Pule barefoot, Freedom with his old plastic shoes, all looking scruffy but me newly showered and changed, we make an odd-looking group. Local people obviously curious, but too polite to ask questions, I take the initiative, telling the woman behind the counter about my support of Andile and Freedom. Coming from miles away these children are nothing to do with her, but she smiles and touches my hand when I tell her the story. As many people do, she wants all children to be able to learn and is glad that I, a stranger, am helping.

Letting her know about writing a book, her delight increases. She likes reading true stories, and tells me: 'You know when you read a book if it is the truth or if the person writing it has made it up.'

One of the pleasures of being in Soweto is people's passion for words, education, learning, books. The dead hands of spin, jargon and corporate-speak long since overtaken the freshness and integrity of language where I live, words are alive again here and of value, as they were thirty years ago. They mean something.

As does the sparse, sometimes careful use of them and

the silences inbetween. As Andile had said simply yesterday 'I have missed you Carol', Freedom said something earlier today which keeps repeating itself in my head.

Sensing it is not *just* the late nights which keep him in bed in the mornings, trying to find out more in the half-asking, half-saying way I have adopted, I had wondered aloud if there was, perhaps, another reason for him not getting up. Freedom had agreed there was, eventually saying in a far-away voice:

'Time is waiting for me.'

Saying no more, looking at me searchingly, he needs to believe I understand him, and I think I do.

His words speak of deep sadness or depression even. He and Andile's lives containable while Isaac was in charge, the withdrawal of their father's firm hand and the long-term absence of a mother means despair gets to Freedom.

Bringing the kotas and drink to eat in the grounds of the Museum, sitting on the semi-circular stone bench next to the boulder, I come back to his words.

'So you are sad sometimes in the morning?' I half-say, half-ask.

Freedom nods. I hesitate. Not wanting to probe too far, to open up something in Freedom I cannot follow through with, I speak instead of my own childhood. His friends chatting nearby, happily tucking into their food, I say how I was a sad child in Africa too. With me it was because with no school to go to I did not have the company of other children. I had no brother or sister at that time and sat by myself doing lessons in a silent room.

Freedom is captivated by this story and, Peace and Pule listening in now, I tell them about Ncema Dam. I speak of the beautiful garden, the loneliness, the animals I adopted when their mothers were shot by the hunter down the track and about Walter, himself a grandfather at that time, me following him around.

I say how I started to write things down so that I would be able to keep people, places, colours in my memory. I kept the sounds of voices too and the sweet smell of wild animals. I speak then of the event in Soweto on June 16th 1976, the Uprising:

'Many children died because they wanted to have an education and to go to school.'

I tell them about the first time I came to this Museum two years ago, how the children's words on the walls came to life in my mind and why this is the place I come to sit every day and to think.

By this time, strolling around, looking at the words on stone, Freedom reading out loud for us the Xhosa version of the event written on the boulder, we have company.

A man wearing a badge, part of a visiting trade union delegation, has been watching our progress and smiles at me:

'Lady, it gladdens my heart to hear you tell these children about this.'

Suddenly it is dark again; 4.30 when we left the house, time has sped by. Once more caught out by the swiftness of nightfall, I am anxious to get back to Neo's. Pointing to the recently full moon Freedom says how much he likes an *orange* moon and do we have one of those in London?

Yes, I say, and it is one of my favourites too. Then, he tells me about learning in science the story of the moon crossing the sun in the UK and there is a word for this which he has been trying to remember.

'Eclipse,' I tell him.

'Ah,' he says. 'Yes. That is the word.'

As we are about to set off, a local woman approaches me: 'Excuse me,' she says sharply 'are these your children?'

Telling her that I am escorting Peace and Pule, two of Freedom's friends, out to tea and about my involvement with Freedom and Andile, her expression changes from one of suspicion to delight. She reacts as the woman at the kota stall did earlier and gives me a heart-warming smile.

We can find no rubbish bin in the Museum grounds to put the paper wrapping from the kotas and the empty drink cans. Carrying them back to Neo's with us, me with the papers, the boys with each of their cans, Freedom touches my arm, takes the bundle from me and collects their empty cans from Peace and Pule. In the dark, his sharp eyes have spotted a bin by the side of the road.

Arriving back, Freedom takes the keys and, as Andile did in the morning, picks the one that fits the lock straight off and opens the gate to let me in.

Whatever demons have beset Isaac, the fact that his sons are good company, courteous and enjoyable to be with, is in large part due to his care. Feeling angry with him on the way in from the airport before meeting him and seeing his plight,

I now feel saddened that he has lost the pleasure of a close relationship with his boys.

Obedient, attentive, funny, this evening Peace and Pule happily dancing all the way down to the Vilakazi, Freedom had watched out for *me*, asking on more than one occasion that I move further onto the verge. Cars can be dangerous he tells me.

Is he over-cautious, I wonder, my mind turning to Isaac's paranoia.

But is it paranoid or real? In a squatter camp, desperate people always wanting to get in, even to these scant dwellings, in a yard near Isaac there has been a bid to push out the existing people and take over their shacks. Finding out about it from Jabu, I have to trust his judgement that Isaac's life and that of his boys are not under threat. I know it will be difficult to help Isaac, for while services like counselling and other forms of emotional help are available, they are vastly over-stretched.

'The boys like you,' Neo says in the kitchen later, without preamble or introduction, after Jabu has taken them home. 'I was watching them in the garden. You can see it in their faces when they look at you.'

I, too, have seen the change in their expressions this year, but I have to do a balancing act between head and heart, I tell Neo. The reality is I live thousands of miles away and must think carefully about how best to be involved, so as not to disappoint them.

'Many families in South Africa live apart from each other because of work and things happening in life,' Neo says.

Part of the generation which remembers fourteen years' exile, the length of her brother's absence from home, she adds: 'So it is not as different as you think, and who will these boys matter to in the way that a mother cares?'

One of the cornerstones of this culture being that a woman's presence is crucial to a child's development and peace of mind, she is suggesting that now they are beginning to know me and I them, I should do what I can.

I understand what Neo means about knowing them. Last year I had ideas about Freedom and Andile, which have changed. I was wrong to think of Andile as the stronger child. They are both now slender children and, yes, I think the world of them. I like the way they are as brothers, close but different people, and am moved by the way they do not demand or even ask. Both hungry this morning, needing breakfast, it was *me* who asked about food. Neo is telling me my care is better than nothing.

Discussing food today, making sure Freedom and Andile had provisions in the house, Freedom it turns out enjoys cooking. Talking animatedly of his liking for vegetables, for spinach, pumpkin and potatoes, he tells me that rice is not his thing. A hand on his stomach, shake of his head, letting me know how it makes him feel bloated.

I wonder if he is cooking the rice properly, but leave it be for now.

Before saying goodbye to Freedom, Peace and Pule tonight I had remembered something. On my last visit Freedom had said he wanted to go into business. It was perhaps a spur of the moment comment and I ask him if he still does.

Yes, he says.

What business would he like to run?

Without hesitation he replies: 'A restaurant.'

When asked why he says:

'Because restaurants, they make a lot of money, and I will always have enough food.'

I have a wish of my own. Both boys picked up a full key-ring today, opened the gate effortlessly, even in the dark. I want to buy them a key-ring each and keys of their own. For that to happen, there will need to be a lock to fit them into, a door for the lock and a house for the door.

Chapter Thirty

Dancing

School dance

Soweto, Saturday 17th September 2005

Jabu letting me know he will be over early this morning to discuss the house, he is beaten to it by Shadrack, the man who had helped design the Hector Pieterson Museum. I have already seen Shadrack to say hello to and now here he is at Neo's kitchen door.

'Carol, do you know French?' he asks breathlessly.

A little. But what does he want, exactly? If it's a document to translate, I can probably help.

No, no, Shadrack shakes his head. It is a large party of

Congolese.

Shadrack, who also runs a tourist firm, has booked to take a group of visitors from the Congo around Soweto. The tour is starting in just over an hour and the French interpreter is nowhere to be found. If my French is up to it, will I take over?

The opportunity to tell friends back home that I, as a white woman, escorted a large party of black people around Soweto, is almost too good to pass up, but my stumbling French is not. Shadrack and I both disappointed that I must turn him down, Neo emerges to help. She thinks there is a French teacher who lives not far away, if only she can remember his address. Ah, but so-and-so will know. Wait, she will find a number.

Jabu then arrives. Drinking tea in the back garden while Neo sorts out Shadrack in the kitchen, he tells me it is not a good idea for Sue and me to come to the builders' yard with him on Monday. 'The price will double if they see a white face,' he says. The same goes for furniture. Jabu says he will be able to strike a better bargain without us.

Disappointed for the second time this morning, first the tour and now being left out of buying things for the house, I see the sense in what is being said. But it leaves me relying heavily on Jabu.

The boys must be involved if the family is to have a chance of recovering and the house needs to be done as quickly as possible, I say. Freedom has already lost school and may be held back a year and Andile is troubled. As the elder child he has suffered more from seeing Isaac lose his grip. If Andile is to be able to take the bigger responsibility for washing, cooking, cleaning, and for taking care of himself and Freedom, he needs a good place to do it. He is only fifteen, after all.

Jabu says he understands and to make the arrangement as clear as we can, I suggest a date of early November for the project to be completed. The home should take no more than two or three days to build, with the family settled well before Christmas and Jabu paid a fee when all is done. He does not want to be paid, but if he is going to take time to organise and oversee the project, it is the only way, I will need to ring to make sure things are happening and I cannot put pressure on him if he is doing the work for nothing.

That agreed, we arrange he will pick me up here in an hour or so and take me to Motsoaledi for a quick visit. Meanwhile, I will walk up to the Museum.

I sit in the grounds writing notes and enjoying what will be some rare peaceful time during this stay in Soweto. Going inside the building I find things have been moved.

Sam's larger-than-life-size picture of Hector, Mbuyisa, and Antoinette is no longer in the foyer. Instead I find it facing me on an end wall up one of the slopes, looking different. Now a square instead of the cropped, oblong photograph it was before, it takes in hundreds of surrounding children who were there that day. Antoinette not at the desk any more, she has moved to working behind the scenes and there are more changes as I read my way once again around the walls.

This time the green Chev is here, in colour. A boy called Steve Lebelo writes that the police went out on the 17th and 18th of June systematically killing people. He pinpoints the 'infamous green car'. Unlike the one in Peter Magubane's book on Soweto, this picture shows the car with five occupants and not a handgun this time, but two long rifles pointing out of the vehicle. It is a cold image, illustrating contempt for those who are being hunted and killed. In the three years the Museum has been open, it is good to see the story expand and include different material as people come forward to add their testimony.

Going out to sit for a while in the sun, the voice of a guide leading a coach party, pointing at Sam's picture of Mbuyisa, Hector and Antoinette on the wall outside, tells us this photograph was taken by Peter Magubane. If you walked a few feet closer, you would see Sam's name on the bottom of it. The tilting, lurching nature of the details of this story does not stop, even here, and as the voice continues, I decide to leave.

Arriving at Motsoaledi, Andile playing football again, Freedom is delighted to see me this morning and, remembering our talk yesterday, asks first thing if I have been to the Hector Pieterson Museum to think. He is thrilled when I answer yes.

I sense he wants to build a narrative between us, a history of things only he and I know about, and he is setting about achieving this. He will do it again when Sue and I come to take him and Andile shopping on Monday afternoon after school. The first thing Freedom will say to me excitedly is 'I bought a kota at school today.' I miss the significance of this for a fraction of a second and Freedom's face is suddenly serious, as if I might have forgotten. It remains anxious until he sees the light go back on in my brain. Recalling the kotas I bought for him, Peace and Pule, 'Ah', I exclaim, 'so you have had another one. Was it the same?'

'Not as big,' he tells me.

Smiling again when he sees I am switched on again, he needs me to remember these links.

Isaac not around again, Andile in a football match, I leave Freedom playing with friends and, back at Vilakazi, decide to pay a visit to Tebello and his wife, Jabu. I am in extra good luck, for Omry is there too.

As before, I find in the company of these three strong people a palpable reason for the Uprising which connects past principles with lives lived now. It shows Lydia, Omry's grandmother's on-going prescence in his passion for conscience and education while Tebello and Jabu continue publicly to denounce the wrongs they see.

Tebello has been talking about it in the papers and on TV and they have a copy of a commemorative programme made for the anniversary of June 16th 2005 for me to take away. He, like Omry, wants ordinary people to be part of democracy and is eager to involve writers.

As Tebello says, 'We have Mandela and Archbishop Tutu, who are both getting old. What will we do when they go?

We will be like a chicken with the head cut off. The body will not know what to do unless it, the body, the people, learn to think for themselves.

'For that to happen we need education for everyone. We need people to be able to use their minds.'

This echoes what some of the trade union delegation had said when I saw them again at the Museum this morning: 'There could be another Mugabe here,' one person commented. 'Many of us, we are very concerned about centralised power in government and the lack of free education.'

Walking down the road with Omry a while later for a chat over another cup of tea, this year he talks about being a father. His younger daughter, Thwanyane, almost two, he is thinking about what kind of parent he is to her and I sit in the restaurant close to Neo's, bemused and happy, as Omry takes the floor. 'You see,' he says, 'as a child you have to know you are loved. That is the first thing. A child shouldn't have to ask if they are loved. They should see it. That is what is missing with lots of parents. They can't find the balance between giving discipline and showing love.'

He says Lydia, his grandmother, had the balance right and tells me that he did not know his own parents loved him. Both working hard, they were very strict and he had to say in his head that they cared. Unlike with Lydia where 'you could see the love in her eyes'.

This talk leading back to Omry's childhood makes me question something about our last meeting and the time has come to tease him about it. He had refused to come out dancing with Manoli and me, but he *does* dance I say. I recall now, he told me he learned ballroom dancing at a youth club when he was a teenager. Have I remembered right?

Bashfully, Omry agrees.

'So have you taken Carol out dancing yet,' I ask?

Omry says they have been busy with the little one. But he will soon.

Well he had better do it before he forgets how.

In all seriousness Omry says that you never forget how to dance. As if to prove the point, his arms begin to form a circle for holding a partner in and I am tempted to get up. Instead, speaking to Carol on the phone a little later, I urge her to promise me something.

Yes, she says, what is it?

'Get Omry to dance.'

Chapter Thirty-One

CAMERAS AND TALKING BOOKS

One of Freedom's pictures

Soweto, Monday 19th September 2005

Sue's eagerly awaited arrival on Sunday evening is followed by a meal and her heading to bed soon after, exhausted from a week's conference and a long drive. We decide to save the serious talk till morning.

Jabu arrives early to drive me to see local MP, Andrew Mlangeni. Arrested the same day as Elias Motsoaledi and serving a total of twenty-six years and four months for his part in the Rivonia plot along with people like Nelson Mandela, he is a modest grey-haired man of medium height and slim build, youthful looking for his eighty years.

Initially we discuss the housing problem in Soweto and elsewhere in South Africa, hundreds of thousands of people living in bleak shanty towns, and he tells me there is little likelihood of resolving this. The poverty of South Africa's neighbours means illegal immigrants from Zimbabwe, Swaziland, Lesotho, Mozambique pour daily across the border, swelling the already overcrowded numbers. He says that until countries like the UK, the US and France recognise this and invest in the neighbouring countries which ring South Africa, people will throng into places like Jo'burg seeking work and the neighbouring townships will suffer.

Switching to June 16th 1976 and the fact that he and the other ANC leaders like Mandela, locked up as they were, did not support the youth, his considered reply depicts both the deadly mis-information which was prevalent and the fear among the old guard, the paranoia even, of letting the youth in.

They had thought, he said, that the young people who marched that day were separatist, wanting to take the country down the 'blacks only' road, which is not what the ANC had planned. The ANC knew they needed the business expertise of white people and their administrative experience as well as their good will to take their country forward. They did not want confrontation with individual whites, but with the system of apartheid.

Ironically, this would seem to prove that the ANC did not organise the March, which is what many ANC stalwarts have claimed retrospectively, and still do, as they see the Uprising attracting world attention.

Andrew Mlangeni concedes it was a mistake to think of Steve Biko and his young followers as pursuing apartheid against whites. It took the elders a long time to recognise the contribution made by Biko's conscientisation movement to helping black people become proud of themselves and aware of their individuality. Due to banning of material, they did not have Biko's first-hand writings to go on and by 1990, when they had all served their lengthy terms, there were other things to attend to.

Obviously regretting the elders' stance, a small chivalrous gesture outside the house reveals his willingness to stand in for a young person now.

Jabu waiting for me in the car, the vehicle has been causing problems and will not start. Jabu in the driving seat, me in the back, Mr Mlangeni puts his shoulder to the door of the car to get it moving. Alarmed lest he harm himself, quickly I get out to try and stop him, but deftly holding the door open with one hand, he manoeuvres me back in with the other: 'You get inside my dear.'

Gesticulating frantically to Jabu to get out, not to let a man more than double his age and half his size push while he sits inside, thank heavens the car starts and Mr Mlangeni waves us goodbye.

Sue, wide awake, breakfasted, chatting to Neo under the gazebo in the back garden when we return, we get down to the business of discussing Freedom, Andile and Isaac. With a lot to catch up on, I tell her what I have discovered as succinctly as possible:

that Isaac is not himself, is either mentally, emotionally or physically ill, possibly all three;
possibly he has taken some kind of substance which has affected his mind and changed him;
he is drinking;
he has infected the boys with a fear for their lives which Jabu says is unsubstantiated.

I add that while Freedom is alert and lively in my company, there is a question mark over whether he is ill, whether his not going to school has some physical cause, and a question mark over Andile's state of mind too, since he now seems the more anxious of the two and has lost weight.

Having given Sue this picture, coming to the subject of the house, I say I think it should be built quickly to help the boys look after themselves, but does Sue feel differently?

No, she says, the place they are in now is dreadful and with the boys growing and needing space, their best chance is to be housed. For the rest, she has an idea. Phoning the administrator of a local charity which works with problem families in Soweto, Sue asks to speak to the main field worker for this area. The woman she speaks to promises she will go to the family as soon as she is able to. She will see Isaac, Freedom and Andile, talk to them, get some medical tests arranged, make an assessment and report back to Sue.

Sue and I next discuss the issue of trying to make sure the three of them are fed and the boys are in school. Clothing for Freedom and Andile will be bought this afternoon, but what about food? While both boys have been clear that Isaac *is* buying food with the money sent, we are both concerned about the drinking and wonder if we should try something else.

Jabu has talked about basic food hampers which shops make up. The opposite of Fortnum and Mason affairs, they contain basic provisions like oil, flour, tea, mealie, sugar, baked beans. Telling Sue about this, by the time Jabu returns after lunch, we have a scheme:

Would Jabu be able to drop off hampers to the household once a fortnight? we ask. I would pay him, through Sue, who instead of sending food money direct to Isaac, would send it to Jabu. As with the house, I would put a small cost on top for his petrol and time. We know the system is not ideal and it may not be the long-term answer, but for now it might work.

That will be fine, Jabu says. He will buy provisions, including taking fresh fruit, meat, eggs and vegetables along from time to time. He will fax Sue the receipts, and she can deposit the money in his bank.

Most of the food taken care of this way, Sue and I agree that Isaac will still have a small amount of money for emergencies and extras.

It is springtime here, mid-September and the birds are nesting. Sitting on the verandah just before lunch, I watch a yellow weaver-bird perch on the slender swaying stem of the red bottlebrush in the corner, look around, perch again on another stem nearby and choose a frond from the edge to take off with. Clamorous cape sparrows and mousebirds fly from the front to the back of the house with beakfuls of straw and dried grass.

People clamour too. Chris, one of the young men who keeps an eye out for Neo's guests, stops me on my walk back from the Museum. He wants to introduce me to a man I have already interviewed who was shot in the leg on June 16th. The latter looking rather sheepish that he has not told Chris we have spoken already, Chris, thinking on his feet, tells me that perhaps the man has more to say.

At this rate, there will be a wardrobe full of clamouring voices in my head, but then you would not take a walk in this part of Soweto without finding people who were on the March or who watched it go by.

Sitting over lunch in the back garden before Jabu picks us up for our afternoon shop, we learn of Neo's thoughts about tourism:

'Look,' she says in disgust, nodding through the wide iron gate from where we can see the road in front, 'Look at what those tourists are doing.'

She is pointing to a vast coach, like a juggernaut, filling the street with its bulk. It is stationary, like a predatory beast, engine growling outside Archbishop Tutu's house fifty yards down the road. The property's modest eight-foot-high stone wall is no match for the vast height of the coach with people standing up inside peering over the top.

As it happens, the house is archbishopless, Desmond and his wife Leah away in Brazil.

Another coach pulling up a short while later, Neo cannot hide her feelings: 'Hasn't he done enough?' she says, referring to Desmond Tutu's long-standing work in his own community and abroad. 'Can't they leave him alone?'

Then, with a strong 'pah' factor in her voice:

'They do not get out, these tourists. People tell them it is too dangerous to get out in Soweto. Those tour guides tell them that.'

Big companies, who are not even based in Soweto, are taking over the market in tourism, she tells us, and local people do not get a look-in. I suggest they lobby to get the road blocked off to big vehicles. But you have another problem if you try and do this, Neo says: vested interest. Someone will be paying someone to let the coaches in.

Sue and I know it is the same the world over, big companies monopolising the world market, making bulky onslaughts on fragile communities, insensible to local people and their lives.

Talking to Jabu about it when he arrives, he tells us 'They [the big companies] pay local people very little. Because there is so much unemployment, they can get away with it.'

Sue and I affected by Neo's distress, the next busload of high-up tourists has us all on our feet. Not sure yet what we will do, the three of us are on the street before we know it, Neo's well-guarded doors and gates wide open behind us.

On the road ahead, the people in the coach are standing up inside their metal fortress with their backs to us, taking pictures of Tutu's empty house.

Sue tells me later she thought of pulling silly faces, Neo is for dancing. I glower. And suddenly, the busload has turned, two white women and a black one have been spotted emerging from a house. Us.

Knowing we are on camera, walking along the short road towards the bus, stopping, turning to each other, Sue and I on either side of Neo, we defer to her as she talks:

'Look at them looking at us,' she says. 'Have they never seen three women talking before?' Our decoy work over, turning round we are glad to get back inside.

Turning to happier subjects on the journey over to Motsoaledi, Sue tells me about an African friend of hers, a woman she had hoped I would meet, but who is away at the moment. Sue met her when she was a cleaner. On the tiny wage she received, Patricia, like her namesake in Motsoaledi, cared about children. She took them in when, orphaned by AIDS, they had nowhere to live. She has a gift for transforming them, Sue says, for enabling them to thrive. I will have to meet her another time.

Freedom and Andile eager for their afternoon shopping trip to Southgate Mall, once there we buy dictionary, ruler, geometry set and a Bible Freedom asks for. Then we go to a shop selling clothes, school uniforms and goods like soap and cosmetics.

Security in shops strict in South Africa, and already with

a bag in our hand, a security guard carefully searches it before we go in. A slender man in his twenties, he is formal and even officious at this stage but quite different when we emerge an hour or so later, Sue and I frazzled. The boys, however, are beaming, Andile having insisted all the clothes go in one enormous bag which he is carrying.

We have bought for both Andile and Freedom a pair of shoes for play, trousers for school, raincoats, which they asked for especially, a sweater each, a pack of grey socks for school, a pack of underpants, swimming trunks, two bars of soap each, deodorant, with Sue making sure they smell it first to see it is the one they like, all of which has come to R630, less than £60.

Sue having reminded me when we were in the stationers, I have bought a yellow birthday card for Andile with balloons on it and a message written inside that I did not forget.

But, in truth, with a memory like the proverbial sieve, and fearful of bringing it back to London in my handbag, I hand it to Andile straight away. I can see how glad he is. 'Thank you for all the things you are buying for us,' he says in his quiet way, but brimful of pleasure on the inside, hardly able to keep in his happiness.

'I care about you both,' I say.

'We know that,' he replies.

The raincoats are smashing, just below knee-length, with hoods and pockets, a black shiny one for Freedom and dark blue for Andile. The swimming trunks are very swell, both the same design, like long shorts, baggy in the leg. Freedom's is mustard yellow and Andile's a lovely shade of muted ochre red. The sweatshirts are a puzzle. Freedom heading straight for a green one, which suits him, turns 180 degrees at close quarters and walks away. Andile does the same with a red and black sweatshirt. The red matching his swimming trunks catches his eye, as it does mine, yet he does not want it.

Ah, so this is it. Close to, they can see the price is R36, just over £3 and, when asked, they say it is too expensive to buy.

This is a special time, I tell them and, for today, they are allowed to have it.

Leaving the shop, Andile proudly carrying the big bag, it is the security guard's turn to get in on the act. Without us realising it, he has been watching us closely, Sue and I 'on camera' for the second time today, but a different kind of photographer this time. For the man has clocked what is going on between these two well-dressed white women and the scruffy boys who are with them.

Having enjoyed what he has seen on his personally shot video of the four of us shopping, and having waited his turn, he now takes centre frame. 'Ah,' he says to Freedom and Andile, hamming it up as he opens the bag wide and pretends to peer intently inside, head moving back and fore, checking what is there. 'What lucky boys you are,' he says eventually, looking up at them and, turning to Sue and me he beams: 'God bless you ladies. Thankyou for doing this for these children.'

We have one last purchase though, a football. Last year's

model long since worn out, the boys dig into a large basket of soccer balls at the sportshop, test them in the air, weigh them in their hands and seem to choose one, yellow with black triangles. But no, this is replaced and they choose another, black and white. Sue spots they have seen the price again and gone for the cheaper model. Taking Andile aside, she asks: 'If you didn't have to think about the money, which one would you choose?' He says the first one, the yellow one, which is what we buy.

We wait while Freedom and Andile take time finding a present for their father. Isaac unshaven at the moment, they go to great trouble and much discussion at the razor counter, choosing one they think will suit him.

Over lunch of pizza for Andile, because he has never tasted pizza before, and chicken and mash for Freedom, we get down to some serious talk about the house, about school, about their difficulties and about the fact that Sue and I will have to leave tomorrow.

I need them to know that although I live a long way away, I think about them and they matter to me. I tell them I will write to them once a month so they know I have not forgotten them. I will find a card with a picture on one side and I will write on the back of it.

'You know how much we care for you both,' Sue takes up the thread, and Andile comes straight in:

'We know this,' he says 'And it makes us very happy.'

We then lay down some ground rules. They must both go to school, otherwise there will be no future for them. We will be making the house happen as quickly as we can and they can phone Sue at any time.

Wanting to phone me too, asking if I have a mobile, they seem to understand that I do not live by mobile phone. I keep it for emergencies, which means it is usually not on. They also understand that London is expensive for them to ring and my landline number is often on ansaphone. When I get back to London, I will try and find a cheaper way to ring them I say, using Siphiwe's number to begin with. The idea suddenly occurs that they could call me on my mobile on Christmas Day. I will leave it on. Both very pleased by this, turning to Freedom I ask what time he thinks he will ring, in the morning or the afternoon.

Considering this for a moment, head to one side, he then grins broadly, looking nine-years-old again. Pointing his smiling face towards me, twisting his shoulders away, 'It will be a surprise,' he says.

Almost dark when we get back, Sue finds Isaac to tell him about the new financial arrangements for the food while I talk to the boys. Standing at the opening of the place which is still their home for now, aware of the oppressiveness inside, we hear a plane fly over in the darkening sky and looking up, see its outline. I tell them I shall be going on one soon, to take me back to the UK and they exclaim how exciting it must be to fly. I tell them I am a little afraid of flying, of being inside a long time, unable to be out in the cool air. I do not use the word claustrophobia, which is what I suffer from.

Both seeming to understand, their faces serious now, 'How long is the journey to London?' Andile asks. When I say eleven hours, 'That is a long time to be inside,' he lets me know.

'With both of you thinking about me, perhaps I will not be frightened?' I half-say, half-ask. They smile.

Sue having had a talk with Isaac, who has accepted the new financial arrangements without demur, shaking hands with him, I say I hope he will find a way of being well. Silent, but nodding his head slightly, a gesture I remember clearly, he is calm on this occasion.

Walking back up the road ten minutes later, darkness fallen, Freedom and Andile are surrounded by dozens of children who come with us to the clearing to say goodbye.

Andile a good head height above the others, Freedom small, I take their hands as they stand in a sea of faces, both of them smiling and unafraid. Wishing to acknowledge that I have a narrative with Andile as well, *our* piece of shared history, I half-ask, half-say something he knows he has already responded to twice today: 'You know Sue and I care about you both?'

He gets the joke, and giggles:

'Yes, Carol. We know that.'

Chapter Thirty-Two

VOICES AND SHAPES IN THE DARK

New house in the making

Tuesday 20th September 2005

Leaving Soweto before 6.30 am, Sue has appointments in Jo'burg and I will make phonecalls on the way, speak again to Freedom's teacher, Charles, and try and make contact with Skipper, his headmaster, who has been in day-long meetings.

My head unreliable without well-planted prompts, it is already in my diary under Christmas Day 2005: 'Switch on mobile.'

After an early start in town, Sue will take us to her brother Paul and sister-in-law Beryl's house for a few days break and a visit to Pilanesberg National Park, before my return flight on Friday.

Larger than Heia, where we had our Iringa reunion two years ago, we will see a one-tusk elephant wandering down the road. A wonderful sight, its fearless presence among the cars causing alarm to drivers, it is in fact taking a short-cut to a small watering hole where we stand and watch it bathing.

Talking with Sue at Neo's the night before, knowing how vulnerable the boys still are despite our arrangements to protect them, she had said: 'You are giving them a chance. In this country, that means a lot.'

Keeping quiet about the fact that I think Freedom and Andile are too young to realise this, Neo reads my thoughts: 'They were brought up differently to you,' she says. 'In this country, if you are given an opportunity to go to school, you know you are lucky.'

The reasons why young people marched are as relevant today as they were thirty years ago. Education is still not free and people's involvement in democracy is discouraged by an inflexible top-down structure which means that, as one man says, 'Your vote means nothing.' The people are indeed still waiting.

My own quest for learning I can trace back to being nine years old in Ncema Dam and wanting to know what the word was for all the space in the middle of things. I was looking for an understanding of 'area', 'space', 'volume'. Knowing about length, width and circles, I wanted Amasi food, the key to how words, numbers and shapes join up. Like the class of '76, I was a child who wanted to go to school.

Needing books as a way of filling the gap, of 'growing my mind', I looked for one that had a lot in it and spotted it one day in the advertising columns of a newspaper in Wales.

Ten years old by now and living with my grandparents while my parents investigated the lie of the land in Tanzania, this book was a one-volume children's encyclopedia containing thousands of pieces of information and pictures too.

Costing twenty-five shillings, my grandparents having no money to buy it, I had saved five shillings from running errands when Great Uncle Gwyn paid us a visit. Talking to me where I sat curled up in an armchair in the front room, I must have told him what my problem was and, straight away there was the answer to it, a pound note on the arm of the chair.

Omry, Tebello, Abbey and Barney's love of education carries with it concern for all children, not just those whose parents have money to pay for books and school fees. It comes from their experience that being allowed to develop your mind is a moral engagement.

My own love of words and books from childhood came about because, in a sense, they saved my life, their uniform presence familiar companions in the corridor that my life sometimes felt like, with its bewildering array of opening and closing doors.

Talking to me about the Uprising, its excitement, momentum and spirit and the fact that he and others found within themselves resources they did not know they possessed, Tebello had said: 'Myself came out of me that day.'

It is what Freire and Biko have written about, the ability to find yourself through language and education, to see and name the world your own way.

The fact that the March changed him, that Tebello says he became his bigger self through taking a moral stance, is something he and others repeat on the commemorative TV programme I watch on video in my London home the following week.

Murphy Morobe and Seth Mazibuko both on the same programme made by SABC1 (South African Broadcasting Corporation) and called *Wednesday*, all who appear on screen, onlookers too, speak the same essential story. The March was orderly, it was for education and against an imposed language, the latter producing, as one ex-pupil describes it, classrooms where all you could hear was the sound of the constant flicking of dictionary pages as pupils tried to catch up with the Afrikaans words.

Speaking to Murphy on the phone, having read the testimonies he and Seth gave to the Truth and Reconciliation Commission, it is not surprising when he tells me the Uprising is as important today as it was then. It matters just as much.

It was not supposed to be, this narrative – the words of the bookshop manager in London – with its voices both deeply silent and clamouring to speak. People in Soweto have paid with their lives for the Uprising's place in history, stored within the memories of those left behind. The story alive and coherent, lit from deep fires in their hearts and minds, shows what is precious and must at all costs be kept. It tells us we are lost, distraught, inconsolable, no one without the company of our minds.

Returning to London, determined to do what I can for Freedom and Andile, I decide my postcards must be regular and sent without fail. I am, to my surprise, guardedly optimistic. Although this trip was hard work, I have begun to know the boys, they have responded to me and small things like the cards may make a difference.

However, I wait as Siphiwe's phone gets lost and his e-mail is on and off. In an era of global communication networks, the fragility of keeping contact with two boys in a squatter camp tests the notion that we live in a joined-up world.

Someone asks the question, 'Why don't they write to you?', to which the answer is that no one who visited where Freedom and Andile presently live would think this possible. There is no room to put clothes or food, let alone paper and pencil.

I had thought I might leave behind a few envelopes with my address on and South African stamps, but this must wait till they have the new house. People in Motsoaledi have said that Sue's and my presence in their lives has affected the boys through their wish to speak English and to find out everything they can about the UK, so I am optimistic it will happen in time.

In another Indian summer in London, temperatures in October at over 20 degrees, I take a trip to Brighton with Ann. Living not far from each other and with a friendship lasting more than fifteen years, we do this sometimes, head for the hills or the sea to have a break and remember what life outside work has to offer. Walking along the Front, sun on our backs, I find my first cards for Freedom and Andile. Both pictures of the sea, one with seashore, a gull and skyline, the other with a distant view of the Pier, I will post them next week.

There are pieces of luck with connections next. Siphiwe's phone comes back from the ether. He has had it on charge for the last few days. No electricity in their houses, some of the mobile phone users in Motsoaledi use an adaptor with a car battery to keep topped up. It just takes time.

But Siphiwe tells me Isaac still keeps Freedom back from school some days. Helping where he can, Siphiwe has been calling Freedom in the morning to get him up. Isaac saying Freedom has already left for school, it is not until Siphiwe sees Freedom later in the yard he finds this is not true. He says I must contact the school again.

Freedom's teacher Charles tells me that Freedom's attendance is indeed intermittent and a second letter has been sent to Isaac asking him to come into school to explain what is going on.

Waiting for this to happen, I have my own idea, far-fetched perhaps, that Isaac may be keeping his younger son back for company, keeping Freedom nearby, like an amulet against loneliness and his own feelings of despair. People do this. They did it in Wales in my childhood, some grandparents, which is the age Isaac is to his sons, feeling their frailty and keeping a younger child at home for companionship and emotional warmth. I believe this is a burden to a child, putting a stop on their playfulness and spontaneity, making them over-solemn, as Freedom sometimes is.

I may never know the reason why Isaac has lost his grip. Nor can I tell yet whether it will remain lost. I am sure from the evidence of my own senses that unemployment played a major role in his crossing an invisible line between survival on one side and loss of dignity and self-respect on the other.

I know I will not get to the bottom of whether the traditional healer he went to was a good person, community minded, or, as seems more likely, one of the charlatans local people say take advantage, setting themselves up in these vulnerable areas to prey on people.

What I will do at long distance, through the postcards, is try and urge Freedom and Andile to be in school and encourage their curiosity about life outside Motsoaledi. Knowing how bright Freedom is, I view his being held back from school with a mixture of frustration, sorrow and despair, but I know too that with help on the sidelines – the someone who puts a pound note on the arm of a chair – he has a chance, the opportunity Sue and Neo spoke of. As this is finished, in November 2005, the visit from the field worker Sue contacted has not yet happened.

Speaking to Charles in mid-November, he gives me the

good news that Freedom is back in school and not asleep at his desk. Sue and I re-arrange the payment for food. Jabu has not been getting through with it and we decide to give the money back to Isaac, but once a fortnight rather than a larger amount once a month.

Having the chance to speak to Andile on Siphiwe's phone, he says how happy he is about this new arrangement because the food has been late a few times and they have been hungry.

'It will be better this way,' he says. 'Our father always buys us food.'

The following week Jabu tells me on the phone the concrete slab for the house has been laid, although an e-mail from Sue saying it is waiting to be laid follows some days later. Jabu being over-stretched is the reason she gives for this hefty slippage. Sue will be visiting in early December, so the evidence had better be concrete by then.

For me, education was life-saving. Not schooling, but the education of 'growing my mind' which initially came from books. As Manoli read Biko in her teenage years, I read whatever I could get hold of: from Solzhenitsyn to Simone de Beauvoir; Wordsworth to Stevie Smith; Shakespeare to T.S. Eliot; Dostoevsky to C.P. Snow, Dylan Thomas and Graham Greene.

By the age of nineteen, beginning a career in journalism, I read material every day: newspapers, magazines, journals, research documents, court reports, minutes of meetings, gradually making sense of the way the world works.

Most importantly, my job gave me access to people:

colleagues in the office and interviews outside. Working in Cardiff at the time, the latter were often with miners and their families in the Rhondda Valley, or people in downtrodden places like Splott.

They were usually survivors: of bad treatment by the then National Coal Board; of blind bureaucracy; administrative blunders; legal loopholes and the rest. A good reading eye, combined with the concern for injustice I share with Sue, with Iringa schoolmates like Linde and with Manoli, leads to 'human interest' and 'investigative' stories being my main fields of work.

A decade or so in newspapers and broadcasting adding its knowledge and weight to childhood experiences, by the age of thirty the adult writer in me has emerged. Fragments from the past, a mix of shapes, colours, scents, flavours, voices knocking at my senses, make journalism not a deep enough channel for all this.

Africa knocked on my senses in a big way, as it does for many who go there: people; clear sounds; soft air; colour; excitement; fear; drama; celebration. None of it in the end could be ignored.

The cause of the schoolchildren who marched on June 16th 1976 is universal. It says no one should dictate to others what should be in their minds and what language they should think in. It says, too, that no one should steal another person's story.

From where I am standing the story is walking down the middle of the road, tilting a bit, but plainly visible all round.

It is wearing a rainbow-coloured uniform from different schools like Belle High Primary, Phefeni Junior Secondary, Morris Isaacson, Naledi High, Orlando West and many more.

Viewed today from both sides of the track, it contains ordinary people's wish for their much-loved country to be well, an almost religious love of the land they were born in and have fought and suffered to bring this far.

Talking in London to a child psychotherapist, she tells me of her work in South Africa with child-led families, children whose parents have died from AIDS. There are thousands of such families where a child of perhaps ten or twelve is the oldest person in a household of younger brothers and sisters.

The community hard-pressed to deal with the practicalities of this, let alone the grief, the therapist tells me how local people themselves try to help. At work all day, finding it is only at night they have time to spare, some visit children when they are asleep and tell them things in the dark. Sitting by bedsides, they tell stories, speak of family histories and give news of the day. When they have said what they need to, they depart, their work completed.

These voices in the dark, the shapes by bedsides, show what people here believe, that whether you are awake or asleep, thinking or dreaming, your life is whole and connected.

Every society needs whole, connected young people coming up behind. It is what education should be for and what story-telling should accomplish. They should include the people arriving next, bring them into the adult circle, embrace them. I have a picture of Omry in mind, sitting at a roadside restaurant, arms reaching out, ready to dance. He has waited since he was sixteen.

He, too, is a child called Freedom, like Tebello, Jabu, Murphy, Seth, Barney, Tsietsi, Mbuyisa, Hector, Antoinette and thousands more.

The freedom they marched for, the brick they took out of the wall, is clear, tangible and on record. The imposition of Afrikaans in schools, deemed to be unworkable, was withdrawn by the following year.

Against all odds, schoolchildren who challenged the apparatus of a long-entrenched tyrannical regime had made an army back down and withdraw its language from their classrooms. In this sense, it was the youth who won the day.

This is a book about connections. The links between Freedom, the class of '76 and me are African childhoods, the wish for narrative and the means to grow and to use our minds.

This is also a book about journeys. The house for Freedom and Andile under way by the end of November 2005, I will return to Soweto next year, keys and key-rings in prospect.

Postscript

Many people have asked if my support of Freedom and Andile is better than giving money through large charities.

The answer to this cannot be Yes. It has been personally and administratively costly, taking the considerable time and expertise of a number of people.

During research I had hoped to find small organisations working on the ground with reliable means of accepting queries and donations. In the time at my disposal this was not possible.

The field is open, of course, for people to find ways of being of value, either through existing charities or personal intervention. Not to be involved would seem the poorer option.

Those who want to assist families in Africa or elsewhere may wish to consider the following:

Siya Phulaphula ('We listen'), a charity run by professionals from the Tavistock Clinic, London, UK, offering a variety of therapeutic work with children and families in South Africa, including training bursaries.

Martin Miller,
11 Thornbury House,
Thornbury Square,
London N6 5YW
(charity no 1089463)

Canon Collins Educational Trust for Southern Africa
22 The Ivories,
6 Northampton Street,
London N1 2HY
UK
Tel +44 (0)20 7354 1462
e-mail ccetsa@canoncollins.org.uk
web www.canoncollins.org.uk
(charity no 1102028)

Medical Campaign for the care of Victims of Torture,
111 Isledon Road,
London N7 7JW
Tel +44 (0)20 7697 7788
web www.torturecare.org.uk
(charity no 1000340)

A website has been set up in the hope of helping children
through involvement with Soweto schools, either through aid
for facilities like musical instruments, or by direct payment
of school fees. This is in progress.

web www.sowetoproject.com.

Acknowledgements

In the UK
this book would not have been possible without Paul Trewhela, who became its enthusiastic ally, and Paddy Donnelly, both of whom provided tremendous assistance and support.

My thanks as well to Hannah Black, Laura Longrigg, Yael Hirson, Alan Clube, Abbey Makoe, Jenny Vaughan, Barry Mackie, Jacob Mothopeng, Patsy Nightingale, Hilary Macaskill, Peter McAdie and Katie Duce.

In South Africa
a big thankyou to Sue Thonell without whose suggestion of visiting Soweto the project would not have begun;

and to Omry Makgoale, Tebello Motapanyane, Skipper, Neo Mamashela, Andrew Mlangeni MP, Shadrack Motau, Charles Radzilani, Tim Couzens, Siphiwe Khumalo, Jane Starfield, Mercy Helms, Jabu Khumalo, the staffs of the Hector Pieterson Museum and the High Commission, Pretoria.

In Spain
my thanks to Manoli Garcia for being such a delightful travelling companion.

In Italy,
where he now lives, warmest thanks to Bill McElroy for his kindness and for the struggles he went through to help the Class of '76.

I am grateful to everyone who agreed to be interviewed and to people in Soweto for their generosity and warmth.

I am especially grateful to the friends and colleagues who contributed towards the house in Soweto for Freedom, Andile and Isaac.

Bibliography

The following books were useful to my research. I have included the date of the edition I read.

Living Apart, Ian Berry, Phaidon, 1996

The Testimony of Steve Biko, Steve Biko, Panther, 1978

I Write What I Like, Steve Biko, Picador, 2004

Soweto, A History, Bonner and Segal, Maskew, Miller, Longman, 1998

A Country Unmasked, Alex Boraine, OUP, 2000

Whirlwind Before the Storm, Brooks and Brickhill, IDAF, 1980

House of Bondage, Ernest Cole, Ridge Press, Allen Lane, 1968

Two Dogs and Freedom, Compilation of children's words, Ravan Press, 1986 (Extract reproduced by kind permission of The Open School)

The Return of the Amasi Bird, Tim Couzens and Essop Patel, eds, Sigma Press, 1982

Banking on Change, Helena Dolny, Penguin, 2001

Truth and Lies, Jillian Edelstein, Granta, 2001

Comrades Against Apartheid Stephen Ellis and Tsepo Sechaba, James Currey Ltd, 1992

Pedagogy of the Oppressed, Paulo Freire, Penguin Educ., 1980 (Extract reproduced by kind permission of Penguin Books Ltd)

The Essential Gesture, Nadine Gordimer, ed. Stephen

Clingman, Jonathan Cape, 1988 (Extract reproduced by kind permission of AP Watt on behalf of Felix Licensing BV and Russell & Volkening Inc.)

The Shackled Continent, Robert Guest, Macmillan, 2004

Liberated Voices: Contemporary Art From South Africa, Frank Herreman, ed., Prestel, 1999

Year of Fire, Year of Ash, Baruch Hirson, Zed Books, 1979

South Africa, R.W. Johnson, Weidenfeld, 2004 (Extract reproduced by kind permission of Weidenfeld & Nicholson)

Country of My Skull, Antjie Krog, Random House, 1998

Call Me Woman, Ellen Kuzwayo, Women's Press, 1985

Black Politics in South Africa Since 1945, Tom Lodge, Ravan Press, 1983

Forced to Grow, Sindiwe Magona, Women's Press, 1992

Soweto, Peter Magubane, Struik, 2001

My Traitor's Heart, Rian Malan, Bodley Head, 1990 (Extract reproduced by kind permission of the Random House Group Ltd and Grove/Atlantic Inc)

Long Walk to Freedom, volumes 1 and 2, Nelson Mandela, Abacus, 2002

Still Grazing, Hugh Masekela, Random House, 2004

Call Me Not a Man, Mtutuzeli Matshoba, Longman, 1979 (Extract reproduced by kind permission of Pearson Education)

Blame Me on History, Bloke Modisane, Thames & Hudson, 1968

Black Theology: The South African Voice, ed. Basil Moore, C Hurst and Co. London, 1973 (Extract reproduced by kind permission of C Hurst and Co)

Down Second Avenue, Ezekiel Mphahlele, Faber, 1971

Out of Bounds, Beverley Naidoo, Penguin, 2001

Fools and Other Stories, Njabulo S. Ndebele, Ravan Press, 1983

History of Southern Africa J.D. Omer-Cooper, Heinemann, 1987

Spirals of Suffering, Brian Rock, HSRC Pretoria, 1997

Mandela, Anthony Sampson, HarperCollins, 1999

The Fifties People, Jurgen Schadeberg, ed., Bailey's African Photo Archives, 1987

A Burning Hunger, Lynda Schuster, Jonathan Cape, 2004

Macbeth, William Shakespeare

A Window On Soweto, Joyce Sikakane, IDAF, 1980

Who Killed Mr Drum?, Sylvester Stein, Corvo, 2003

Soweto Stories, Miriam Tlali, Pandora, 1989

Mbokodo: A Soldier's Story, Mwezi Twala and Ed Benard, Jonathan Ball, 1994

Biko, Donald Woods, Penguin, 1987

Robben Island, D.M. Zwelonke, Heinemann, 1973

Searchlight South Africa, nos. 1–12, 1988–1995

Extract from the *Independent* reproduced by kind permission of the *Independent*

Extract from the *Mirror* reproduced by kind permission of the *Mirror*

Extract from the Museum and its Precincts reprinted by kind permission of the Hector Pieterson Museum, Soweto

Quotation from *South Africa: There is no crisis*, Thames

Television 1976, reprinted by kind permission of Freemantle Media Ltd.

Photograph on page 110 by kind permission of Sam Nzima